Women With ADHD

A Life-Changing Guide to Embrace the Hidden Struggles of Living with ADHD – Includes Debunked Myths and 15 Effective Tips to Positively Transform Your Life

Roberta Sander

1

Table of Contents

Introduction

ADHD does not distinguish between the sexes. It can occur in women as often as it does in men. There is a tendency for ADHD to go undiagnosed in women, but men are more likely to receive a clear diagnosis during their lifetime. Studies show that misdiagnosing a woman with ADHD is more likely to occur because symptoms of this disorder present themselves differently in women than in men. Whereas symptoms in men exhibit as the stereotypical ones, symptoms in women tend to be more subtle and do not necessarily become obvious until something drastic and "unwoman-like" happens.

Oftentimes, when women are misdiagnosed with ADHD, they may attribute their symptoms and behavior to another condition, consequently failing to get the help they need. They have probably not realized they have ADHD to begin with to talk of coming to terms with it. This puts women with this disorder in a vicious circle of them not getting the proper treatment and the right help they need. This may lead to self-destructive behavior, especially when one is receiving treatment for the wrong condition. Women with ADHD may find it very hard to live up to the stereotypical woman figure in their society, especially when they are not diagnosed or are misdiagnosed. This can often cause depression and anxiety because they fail to fit in society for reasons that would still be unexplained and unknown to them until they are diagnosed. Although not every woman who fails to fit the stereotypical figure created by society does so due to an undiagnosed or misdiagnosed mental health disorder such as ADHD, many women with undiagnosed ADHD can find it hard to abide by these stereotypes. How society thinks a woman should behave varies from one society to another, and although some independent women have no one to answer to in their daily lives, they still impose expectations on themselves based on the society they live in.

You might feel like you are inconsistent in your daily tasks or feel like you are falling short of expectations. It might feel like your life overall is too much! You might struggle to succeed or feel overwhelmed at times. There are ways to overcome this or, better yet, live in harmony with one's state of ADHD. This book is not to help you use this condition as an excuse to opt out of living your fullest life but rather to help you and the people around you to better understand why you feel some particular emotions or do certain things. Your closest friends and family can once and for all know why you act the way you do and why sometimes you find it hard to keep up with commitments you have taken up impulsively. They can be there with you to support you and help share your load. Your inner circle of people can become more compassionate and understanding of you and your actions. You can eventually stop hearing the things you do not want to hear as a woman with ADHD! Learning how to say "Maybe" before you say "Yes" can help take away that nagging feeling that you should be capable of doing more or performing better.

Reducing the number of commitments in one's life can help relieve the load on your schedule and will also help de-clutter your life. Women are often expected to be the organizers and planners for themselves and their families. They tend to commit to tasks leaving no time for themselves. It should be acceptable to assign tasks you are not good at or share duties you are not capable of completing on your own. There are plenty of tools that a woman with ADHD can utilize to help make their lives more manageable, and this book will outline just that. Women should learn to love themselves and understand that one is born with value rather than judging oneself based on the expectations put on them.

I will define ADHD and talk about the different types, including the most common signs and symptoms to look out for. Understanding the condition can help you understand yourself. ADHD can affect your relationships, your sleeping patterns, your emotions, and your sexuality. Hormonal changes and aging can cause symptoms of ADHD to worsen, making performing daily tasks an even bigger challenge. Although you might find yourself in the depths of despair at times, do keep in mind that there are certain jobs that women with ADHD perform better than those that do not have ADHD, your focus can be improved, and physical activity can help your state of ADHD. There are effective ways to cope with your ADHD, and yes, you can stop constantly losing things! Diagnosing a woman with ADHD can not only change their perception of themselves but help them cope with this condition throughout their lives. How can you instigate change without finding the root cause, right? If you are a woman with ADHD, you might have realized by now that there is no cure for this condition, but there are ways to manage it to enable you to live your best life; I can't stress this enough.

Just know that as a woman with ADHD, it all boils down to first getting you properly diagnosed then putting you on the right treatment. Everything else will follow through.

Chapter 1:
What is ADHD?

ADHD is short for Attention deficit hyperactivity disorder. This is a mental health condition that mostly affects children, but because it often lives up into adulthood, it significantly affects adults as well. This condition mainly affects people's behavior and often makes the sufferer look like they are restless and find it hard to concentrate or often act impulsively. People with ADHD might come across as having above-average levels of energy and may find it very hard to focus or sit still for long periods of time. The differences in brain development and brain activity of people with ADHD affect their attention levels and self-control. Tedious activities that require sustained attention over a long time might be difficult for people suffering from ADHD unless it is something they absolutely enjoy doing and will voluntarily engage in.

ADHD is not the result of poor parenting skills, excessive sugar consumption, or a lot of screen time, and it can be hard to explain this to non-sufferers. I think it is fair to say that everyone has, at some point, forgotten to turn in an assignment, misplaced their keys, or spaced out during a conversation. What sets someone with ADHD apart from someone without is how frequent these incidents are. When someone with ADHD does these things, it is very easy to assume this is normal behavior since people who do not have ADHD do them as well. If someone with ADHD misplaces stuff all the time, shows up late for appointments, or often seems spaced out during conversations, they might come across as careless, not being time-conscious, or inattentive to those who do not have a clear understanding of ADHD and what it is. Behavior is affected by the brain. ADHD brains develop and function much differently than neurotypical brains. If you are surrounded by the right support system, the attributes of a brain with ADHD can be extremely beneficial in certain situations; otherwise, they can be highly debilitating for the sufferer and those around them. Although AD stands for attention deficit, it does not necessarily mean people with ADHD showcase a lack of attention but rather find it difficult to regulate their attention or shift it onto the right task. Think of a brain that is jumping from one thing to the next or, the other extreme, hyper-focusing on one task. The executive function system of the brain acts like the self-management system helping to plan, prioritize and distribute efforts over different tasks. This internal system will help one inhibit their impulses and only switch from one task to the next when appropriate. These executive functions tend to develop slower in brains with ADHD. People with ADHD tend to have a deficit in certain brain chemicals that help them function this way, like norepinephrine. This is a chemical in the body that should be a naturally occurring one. Norepinephrine, also known as NE, is a neurotransmitter that helps send signals between one nerve cell to the next. The deficiency or lack thereof can cause ADHD. NE usually bonds to dopamine, another chemical messenger in the body primarily responsible for feelings like pleasure, motivation, memory retention, and attention. It also helps in planning and thinking. An ADHD brain has an impaired neurotransmission activity in four functional regions of the brain: frontal cortex, Limbic system, Basal ganglia, and the reticular activating system. The frontal cortex is responsible for attention and organization. The limbic system is located deep inside the brain, and it helps regulate attention and emotions. The basal ganglia are found within the cerebral

9

hemispheres and are tasked with our motor control functions, behavior, and emotions. The reticular activating system maintains consciousness, motivation, and arousals associated with behavior.

Those with ADHD tend to have an even more limited working memory than those who do not suffer from ADHD, making a simple task even more challenging, like reading the steps of a recipe and following through without referring to it multiple times. Following multistep directions can be very hard to keep up with when you have ADHD, and it is perfectly understandable to rely heavily on post-it notes; they are helpful!

Not everyone with ADHD is hyperactive. You might not see ADHD sufferers bouncing around the room, but their brain might be; you just cannot see it. This is described as internal restlessness, and it can be very exhausting. Think of a mind constantly going around in a hamster wheel, like your brain being put in a ping-pong machine.

When energy is directed well, besides being beneficial, it can also be seen as creativity, curiosity, and drive. Before someone with ADHD takes advantage of their brain's strength and capabilities, they must learn to manage and control their energy. People with ADHD not only have difficulty regulating attention but also controlling their emotions. This is often referred to as emotional dysregulation. People with ADHD who have trouble regulating their emotions can come across as being too sensitive.

Both adults and children with ADHD may find it difficult to concentrate on tasks presented to them either at work or school. Some confess they often find themselves daydreaming. Adult ADHD sufferers may make rushed decisions that will, in turn, adversely affect their lives. Scientifically ADHD displays alterations in the brain's growth and overall development. Everybody has trouble keeping still, paying attention, or suppressing impulsive behavior from time to time. However, for some people, the issues are so prevalent and constant that they affect every part of their life: home, academic, social, and employment. ADHD is distinguished by developmental abnormalities in inattention, impulsivity, and hyperactivity. Individuals with ADHD can achieve great success in life. However, if ADHD is not identified and treated properly, it may have negative repercussions such as lack of performance at school, family tension and disturbance, depression, marital troubles, drug abuse, delinquency, unintended accidents, and failure at work. Early diagnosis is crucial.

When symptoms of ADHD are perceived as personality defects rather than an actual mental health condition, it can be hurtful to those going through it; this causes sufferers to believe that it is a personality defect, which affects their self-esteem and leads to other conditions such as anxiety and depression. Can you imagine being the most motivated, the laziest, the smartest, and the stupidest all at one go? It can be very confusing for the sufferer and misleading for those around them. This can be avoided if the person suffering from ADHD, and others around them, acknowledge and understand the constant struggles one faces and, together, find strategies to help overcome these challenges. Eventually, people with ADHD stop beating themselves up about these flaws and focus on the more important things like finding their strengths.

Chapter 2:
What are the different types of ADHD?

A DHD starts off affecting children, but it is possible to develop late-onset ADHD, with certain signs and symptoms being present in childhood, although gone unnoticed.   It is therefore considered to be a chronic condition. ADHD exists in three different major types: inattentive type, hyperactive-impulsive type, and the combination type. For someone to identify which type of ADHD they suffer from, they would have to analyze their symptoms. Someone is considered to have ADHD not only when they experience some of the symptoms we are yet to discuss but when these symptoms start to affect their day-to-day life. Symptoms might not always be consistent, and one might experience various symptoms over time that would pertain to all three types of ADHD.

ADHD is mainly characterized by inattention, hyperactivity, and impulsive behavior overall. Inattention means you get distracted very often and possess poor concentration and organizational skills. Impulsivity means you take risks and often interrupt while someone else is talking or doing something. Hyperactivity is often depicted as never slowing down, fidgeting, constantly talking, and having difficulty staying on one task.

Although many specialists in the field have identified numerous types of ADHD, we will be looking only at the major types and helping to identify them according to their symptoms.

The inattentive type-

If you have this type of ADHD, you experience inattention more frequently than you would impulsivity or hyperactivity. You still struggle with these at times, but they would not be the main symptoms you exhibit. If you have this type of ADHD, you miss details or get distracted easily. You have trouble focusing on a single task and often are reluctant to do tasks requiring a sustained mental effort. On the other hand, people with this type of ADHD fixate on activities that do not require mental effort, such as watching television. You also have trouble organizing your thoughts and learning new information. The inattentive type tends to misplace or lose valuables such as house keys, phones, or other important things required to complete tasks such as pencils or papers. Although this happens involuntarily, people with this type of ADHD might seem like they are not listening or appear to be daydreaming during a conversation. Some might process information much slower, while others misinterpret it. People with this type of ADHD have trouble following directions or instructions. They also have poor organizational and study skills appropriate for their age and tend to be forgetful and miss attending to details. People with this type of ADHD tend to come across as making careless errors. There is a tendency for girls to be diagnosed with this type of ADHD more than boys, and it also prevails in older children and adults rather than younger ones. Children with this form of ADHD have trouble paying attention. They have disrupted concentration but do not suffer from impulsivity or hyperactivity. This is often referred to as attention-deficit disorder informally because the hyperactivity part is not present. Since they are not noisy in class, children with this form of ADHD can go unnoticed. They can seem shy or "daydreamy" in reality. They may not have major behavioral issues. However, their concentration issues can continue to cause them a great deal of trouble.

The hyperactive-impulsive type-

Although people with the hyperactive-impulsive type of ADHD tend to showcase signs of inattention, is it not the main characteristic. Often people with this type of ADHD experience symptoms of impulsivity and hyperactivity. They tend to fidget, feel restless, and have difficulty simply sitting still. They often move around without an apparent goal besides just being in motion. Some may play with or touch objects even when inappropriate or unrelated to the task at hand. Hyperactive-impulsive ADHD sufferers tend to have trouble engaging in quiet activities and are often impatient. As the term itself implies, some may act out and do not think about the consequences of their actions. They may also pass inappropriate comments and blab out answers without giving it a second thought. They may finish other people's sentences unintentionally. People with this type of ADHD may have temper outbursts. Children and adults with this type of ADHD may hinder the learning process for themselves and others in a classroom setup. This is the least common type of ADHD and is more prominent in men and boys. This type is most often found in very young children. This form of ADHD is frequently easier to detect because of the constant moving about.

The combination type-

This type of ADHD will have sufferers display different symptoms that do not exclusively fall within one category or the other. A combination of both categories characterizes this type of ADHD. Almost everyone, including non-ADHD sufferers, at some point, experience some degree of inattentiveness or impulsive behavior, and I am not referring to that recent expensive purchase you made from the mall recently, justifying it as impulse-buying. These characteristics are more severe in people with ADHD to a point where it interferes with their lives, how they function at home, school, work, and in social situations. If you have this type of ADHD, you probably also have a short attention span. This type of ADHD is also the most common. You are easily distracted and often forgetful. You interrupt others more than you should and often act without thinking things through. Besides fidgeting excessively, you probably come across as a chatterbox. You also lose things more often than you should. Children with this form of ADHD have serious issues with hyperactivity and impulsivity as well as inattention. However, when they enter adolescence, they may become less impulsive.

Studies show that ADHD affects different parts of the brain, primarily the prefrontal cortex and the cerebellum. These areas are affected by dopamine, serotonin, and GABA neurotransmitters, short for gamma-aminobutyric acid. Areas of the brain, like the frontal lobe, control the executive function, memory, understanding, emotional impulses, mood stability, and visual processing. The basal ganglia are large structures deep in the brain that help generate the neurotransmitter dopamine; and the limbic system, which sets emotional responses. These are all affected parts of the brain mainly looked at in neurodiverse individuals to help determine which type of ADHD they have and what their symptoms are. Scientists who divide ADHD into further sub-types often look at the symptoms and their cause to prescribe the right treatment. Usually, they focus on the neurotransmitter deficiency and how that can be compensated.

For instance, apart from the three types mentioned above, some believe that there is an over-focused type of ADHD caused by dopamine and serotonin deficiencies. People with this type of ADD, also known as attention deficit disorder and does not include hyperactivity symptoms, as the name implies, will have trouble shifting from one task to the next and are often stuck in negative thoughts, disrupting their progress in life and causes them to have poor sleeping patterns. Some believe that supplements can help treat this specific type of ADD by taking saffron, 5-HTP supplements, and L-tryptophan. A low protein diet is also suggested in this instance. Researchers believe that magnesium can also help with aggressive behaviors, anxiety, and irritability if you have temporal lobe ADD, which usually displays classic ADD symptoms and behavioral problems. Some researchers go as far as dividing ADHD into seven types rather than three; however, these include the main three types, and this all depends on their approach, experience, and research in the field. The resources they have to diagnose ADHD also determine whether they go by the three main types of ADHD. Diagnosing also depends on the country and the guidelines given to professionals in that area. For example, the US uses the DSM5, which is the Diagnostic and Statistical Manual of Mental disorders, while Europeans go by the guidelines given by the European Psychiatric Association.

If they have access to brain imaging, they may be able to further their diagnosis, but family doctors and physicians can diagnose ADHD using general guidelines and clinical assessments.

Chapter 3:
Common Signs you need to know

Women will often live their lives with undiagnosed ADHD mostly because they have been taught to believe this condition only affects men. Women, like I've already said, tend to exhibit lighter symptoms of ADHD, mostly the inattentive type, unlike men who usually showcase symptoms attributed mostly to behavior and tend to be more hyperactive and impulsive. Women may find it hard to focus or pay attention to detail. They may struggle to stay organized or even remember the simplest of things. Active listening can also be a hard task for women with ADHD. Instead of diagnosing women with ADHD, one might be perceived as spacing out, chatty or forgetful. Once these women pluck up the courage to reach out for help, they might even be diagnosed with anxiety or depression instead.

If you have been told to fall silent or pull yourself together more times than you can remember, you should probably stick around to read the rest of this. If you have been told to be more punctual and stop misplacing things, or at some point have secretly wondered if you have ADHD, you should stick around too. If you have been to a professional only to be misdiagnosed or feel like the treatment you are receiving is barely helping you, you would probably benefit from keeping an eye out for the common signs and symptoms you need to know about when it comes to suspecting ADHD. The symptoms you detect must be present in two or more environments, much like having two variables but consistent results. Most of these symptoms would have been present in one's childhood but overlooked the entire time.

In this day and age, it is safe to say that many things are designed to get our attention, like pop-up ads, billboards, and social media in general. If you fall for these almost every time, it does not mean you do have ADHD, and that is why you must also have more than just a handful of these forthcoming symptoms and in different environments, to a point where it is interfering with your daily routine. Your symptoms might include:

- Failing to pay close attention to detail, making careless mistakes, and producing inaccurate work or have been told to push through and be less careless.
- Finding it difficult to sustain attention during assigned tasks. You may find yourself constantly writing notes during a lecture because if you are not always engaging your senses, your mind will trail off.
- Checking out of conversations unintentionally or finding it hard to complete lengthy reading. Your mind may seem to be elsewhere even in the absence of an obvious distraction, kind of like daydreaming.
- Finding it difficult to follow through on instructions, directions, or some of the simplest of tasks like doing the laundry. You may get easily side-tracked.
- Finding difficulty in organizing tasks, activities, or belongings.
- Poor time management and failure to meet deadlines- You might be perceived as chronically late because you always assume you have more time available than you actually have. You might have even stood your friends up or picked up your kids late from school.

- Avoiding or feeling reluctant to engage in tasks you know will require sustained attention. You may find it hard to study or to engage in a subject you are not interested in. Reviewing lengthy articles or filling of forms can become a challenge.
- Often losing or misplacing necessary things such as diaries, home keys, wallet, or phones. Some might often find themselves trying to be productive out of a cluttered desk or workstation.
- Being easily distracted by external stimuli like background noises while you struggle to concentrate on one particular task.
- Forgetting to complete daily activities, like not returning calls or overlooking daily appointments.
- Seeming uneasy, fidgetting, or constantly tapping your finger or feet.
- Leaving your seat in inappropriate situations like during class or a meeting
- Climbing or running in inappropriate situations, mostly present in children. It may be depicted as feeling restless in adults.
- Being unable to engage in leisure activities such as yoga classes. Meditating can be difficult to complete if you have ADHD. In cases of children, they might be unable to play or engage in games with their peers.
- Often being perceived as always on the go and never easy-going. You may find it hard to relax and always want to work on a million things.
- Talking excessively and being thought of as a chatterbox.
- Babbling out answers before a question is even completed. You may complete people's sentences before they even finish.

Although people with ADHD may come across as rude when doing this, they do this unintentionally.

- Finding difficulty in waiting your turn in lines or queues.
- Interrupting or intruding on others like butting in conversations, games, or tasks.
- Constantly feeling exhausted and overwhelmed.
- Finding yourself constantly taking care of other people and their duties and rarely taking care of yourself and your own needs.
- Constantly comparing yourself with the people around you or your idols on social media and often getting disappointed with the result. This may make you feel inadequate or subpar. You may try to overcompensate by striving to be more organized or be more put together. This may result in other co-existing conditions like eating disorders or sleep issues.
- Having lower self-esteem levels than neurotypical women.
- Experiencing more depression, anxiety, and stress when compared to neurotypical women.
- Becoming more emotionally oriented rather than task-oriented, like coming across as overreacting, freaking out, or even freezing in certain situations.
- Finding it difficult to simply say "No" and biting off more than you can chew. You feel responsible for taking over new tasks, although you are perfectly aware you already have so much on your plate and would be better off refusing any more responsibilities.
- Emotional dysregulation. Finding it hard to control or tolerate frustration, be less patient, and finding it hard to plan or organize oneself.

- Feeling incompetent and unable to perform tasks others might complete effortlessly.
- Finding it hard to make the simplest of decisions and struggling even more to make a final ruling for more important life decisions.
- Finding it hard to hold a job or not getting in trouble at work, to begin with.
- Finding it hard to stay motivated to accomplish your set goals.
- Finding it hard to follow a pre-set schedule that has been set out for you. You would rather work late at night than having to start work early in the morning like the rest of your co-workers.
- Feeling psychologically distressed or inadequate.
- Devoting a lot of time trying to look normal and fit in with the norm.
- Avoiding social events like attending parties because you feel shy or find it difficult to interact or make new friends.
- It may be hard to keep up friendships because social rules may seem complicated to you or you have a hard time following them.
- May fall behind with bills.
- You tend to compensate for your shortcomings with expensive gifts. If, for example, you forgot your best friend's birthday, you buy them an extravagant gift to make up for your forgetfulness.
- Trips to the mall may give you a momentarily feel-good vibe, but you often regret it when you realize how much you have spent.
- A trip to the grocery store takes a toll on you because you find it hard to decide which chocolate or pasta to buy.

- Although you always spend more time at the grocery store than you should, you still manage to walk out of there forgetting one item you absolutely told yourself not to forget when you walked in there.
- If your house is cluttered, you will be embarrassed when family and friends come to visit you, rather than enjoying the time you have with your loved ones.
- You come across as a rebel because you do not fit the stereotypical women figure in your society.
- You feel like shutting down in the middle of the day.
- Spending most of your day trying to cope or looking for things you have misplaced.
- You often feel like life, in general, is too much and find yourself trying to constantly meet the demands of others.
- You might have great ideas but fail to work on them, plan or organize them.
- You spend most of your energy trying to cope, stay organized and hold things together without leaving anytime for relaxation.

Chapter 4:
How to diagnose ADHD in women

W omen with ADHD tend to have the inattentive type of this disorder, as said before. There would be, of course, women who have the hyperactive-impulsive type, which will get these women diagnosed earlier in life as the symptoms they exhibit are more commonly associated with ADHD. Imagine giving a woman the responsibility to take care of her family and kids over and above the duties she has already been assigned, like pursuing a career. They already struggle with organizing and taking control over their life; any further duties would be too much. This places an even bigger burden on women with ADHD, and they often come across as the ones that do not perform well enough.

Like men, women with ADHD have issues self-regulating themselves and often fall victim to peer pressure. They are more likely to experiment with sex, alcohol, or drugs. Because symptoms of ADHD in women are more subtle, they are often confused with personality traits. Young girls or female adolescents might be less disruptive in school compared to boys, so their condition may remain undetected. During puberty, young girls get increased estrogen levels which consequently causes their ADHD symptoms to worsen. Some girls may have never experienced or displayed symptoms of ADHD until their adolescent years, making this a big contributor to late diagnosis.

There is a strong link between ADHD and other conditions. There is no arguing; ADHD places a mental strain on the sufferer, which may lead to other disorders like anxiety, obsessive-compulsive disorder, depression, bipolar disorder, sleep disturbances, and eating disorders. Early diagnosis of ADHD can substantially improve the lives of these women. Professionals tend to get side-tracked by other co-existing conditions and fail to diagnose the root cause of their symptoms.

Healthcare professionals can take various approaches to diagnose ADHD. There is no right or wrong test for this, and often, a psychiatrist or a therapist will diagnose you after a series of assessments. Guidelines ask specialists to also consider the severity of the condition. This varies depending on how it manifests itself over the course of a person's life. Clinicians may categorize ADHD intensity as mild, moderate, or severe. Mild can mean that few symptoms are present, and these symptoms minimally impair the sufferer in a social setting, at school, or at work. Moderate ADHD means symptoms have a functional impairment and are usually more powerful than those presented in mild cases of ADHD. Severe ADHD can mean symptoms are present heavily and are highly interfere with one's life at work, in a relationship, at school, or at home. Individuals' symptoms can diminish, improve, or take on new forms as they mature. Adults that retain any but not all of the signs of childhood ADHD can be diagnosed with ADHD in partial remission.

Diagnosing adult women with ADHD varies from diagnosing young children, so is the diagnostic approach taken by clinicians. The specialist gathers more information from you about your present symptoms. At present, clinicians are guided to verify whether symptoms were present in childhood; if otherwise, a confirmed diagnosis of ADHD cannot be given. If this cannot be confirmed because someone may be unsure about signs and symptoms present years ago, the specialist might want to review your school records, speak to your previous teachers, and consult your parents or guardians. For a definitive diagnosis to be made, one must display effects of their symptoms during their day-to-day activities, such as dangerous driving, underachieving at work or school, struggle to maintain friendships and relationships. Questionnaires and psychological tests are also performed by a specialist to help diagnose ADHD. At present, guidelines indicate one must have at least five or more symptoms to be diagnosed with ADHD, and these symptoms must interfere with their day-to-day living. In adults, symptoms need to be traced back to childhood, and your therapist or specialist will help you identify these issues from the past. In the clinic room, you will also identify how often these symptoms appear and in which settings do they often exhibit.

Because ADHD traits tend to be hereditary, some adults find out about their own state of ADHD after their children get diagnosed. You may also be subject to attention-span tests and other checklists. During the assessment, it will be determined whether the sufferer has any co-occurring conditions or if the symptoms mistaken for ADHD are being caused by another disorder. Besides gathering additional information from others around you, the clinician will perform a behavior-rating scale to help compare behaviors of people with ADHD and others without. After gathering enough information, it might be required to perform further tests based on the results already achieved. A medical examination will also take place to rule out any medical causes for the symptoms. Diagnosing ADHD can start with a simple visit to your primary healthcare practitioner, although it will likely not end there. As complex as it is, ADHD might be hard to diagnose if a general practitioner is not trained enough or does not have the right tools to help diagnose you. It is a first step in the right direction, and when outside their capabilities, doctors often refer you to different specialists. Diagnosing adults with ADHD can be trickier than diagnosing children because general guidelines tend to be more targeted towards children rather than adults and because symptoms in children may be more prominent.

A diagnosis in adult women is mostly made from the individual's history, but other methods may be used, such as continuous performance tests, checking for impulsivity or attention problems, and brain scans. Social, medical, and family history are all assessed during one-on-one consultations with your clinician. This will help determine the challenges you seem to face in your life and underlying medical conditions that may be mistaken for symptoms of ADHD. Completing an ADHD rating scale test will help determine whether an adult has ADHD and if they also have other issues like learning disabilities, auditory disorders, or mood disorders. These tests may take from a couple of hours to multiple days, depending on the clinician's approach and the extent of the condition. An intelligence test may also be performed to test one's IQ and help identify other learning disabilities. If a mood disorder is suspected, a broad-spectrum scale test may also be performed to help identify other emotional or psychiatric problems such as obsessive-compulsive disorder. Depending on the outcome of these tests, one might opt to perform other specific tests to test abilities like motor skills or memory recall. Computer tests for ADHD are also becoming a trend, primarily because sufferers enjoy taking them. These will screen them for impulsivity and attention problems. Continuous performance tests, known as CPT, challenge people to maintain attention throughout. Targets will appear on the screen, and the users need to respond to these targets. The system records their ability to stay on task.

It has been revealed that certain parts of the brain have different imagery, with the help of Positron emission tomography (PET) scans, single-photon emission computed tomography (SPECT) scans, and Magnetic resonance imaging (MRI), than those suffering from ADHD when compared to those that do not have ADHD. These scans are carried out to help monitor and identify the brain's activity and blood flow in certain parts of the brain.

This will reveal areas of the brain that function at normal levels, other areas that work too hard, and others that do not work hard enough. Because every part of the brain is responsible for different functions, these scans can help pin down symptoms attributed to low or high activity of specific areas of the brain that contribute to the overall diagnosis of ADHD. It is proven that ADHD brains mature slower than neurotypical brains. This delay usually occurs in the frontal lobe of the brain. This is responsible for impulse control, focus, attention, and planning. When diagnosing ADHD, it is important to look not only at behavior but also at how different parts of the brain communicate with each other. Women with ADHD may also exhibit symptoms related to behavior, cognitive issues, and motivational functioning. Both brain structure and activity are important for ADHD diagnoses. Another biological test used to diagnose ADHD is the neuropsychiatric EEG-based assessment aid. This monitors the number and type of brain waves nerve cells emit each second. ADHD brains tend to have higher brain waves when compared to neurotypical brains. Getting a high score on this test will not necessarily mean you have ADHD. It can indicate you may have suffered head trauma in the past, substance abuse, or auditory-related disorders. This test is not the sole testing tool for ADHD, but it can be used alongside other clinical tests and examinations.

Diagnosing ADHD is purely based on a clinical evaluation as there are no laboratory-based tests that will help diagnose ADHD, such as blood tests. Different physicians can have different approaches to diagnosing ADHD, and this can depend on their resources and their preferred methods.

All in all, taking the first step in the right direction, as I've said previously, is what matters the most. Seeing your trusted practitioner is all it takes to get you started and eventually getting you the help you need.

Chapter 5:
What Happens to Women with ADHD Left Undiagnosed?

Missing a diagnosis for any condition can be devastating for one's physical and mental health, including ADHD. By now, we have very well established why and how women are mostly undiagnosed or misdiagnosed with ADHD more often than men. Women will get a diagnosis mostly when they enter adulthood and start taking up heavier responsibilities like running a family or working a career. This may result in frequent trips to the psychiatrist, only to be told they have depression or anxiety and be treated for these conditions; however, they would notice that the problem remains.

Women with undiagnosed ADHD tend to have different manifestations than men, such as eating disorders, anxiety, depression, and low self-esteem, as extensively discussed. The inattentive type of undiagnosed ADHD in women can result in teen pregnancy, higher rates of dropouts in school, and a higher risk of getting fired from their job. Undiagnosed women may be prone to more frequent career changes. If you have been misdiagnosed with ADHD or not diagnosed at all, you may tend to let your bills go unpaid and not running errands properly. A series of these events leave women feeling disappointed because they are not completing tasks as expected of them.

Women with undiagnosed ADHD may experience rejection-sensitive dysphoria, also known as RSD. This is an emotional sensitivity and pain usually triggering a notion of rejection and criticism caused by the most important people in one's life. This can also be caused by a sense of failing to meet expectations or unable to fulfill standards either imposed on oneself or imposed by others. This does not mean that ADHD sufferers with RSD are too sensitive or unable to handle criticism but rather have an amplified emotional response compared to people without this condition. No one likes criticism or that feeling of rejection; however, people with ADHD and RSD have a more severe reaction to criticism, and this may highly impair their lives. Because the emotional response of RSD is internalized, it will often be portrayed as a mood disorder, with occasional suicidal ideation. Think of someone who is feeling perfectly fine at a given moment and immensely sad in the next. This results in diagnosing individuals with cycling mood disorders rather than ADHD. It might take time for clinicians to make a correct and accurate diagnosis in these instances because RSD is very common in adults with ADHD. This emotional response can also be externalized, often seeming like instant rage towards the person responsible for causing such emotional pain.

RSD in women with ADHD may make sufferers anticipate rejection even when it is not likely to happen. They may also be on the lookout for avoiding such feelings all together resulting in social phobia. Women with ADHD who also experience RSD may describe this feeling as overwhelming and often triggered by fear of loss, approval, and love from others around them. Women with undiagnosed ADHD may cope with this differently, but it mainly boils down to two ways. They may become people-pleasers and present a false version of themselves, hoping to feel accepted and be liked by those around them. This may become such a big focus of their lives that they forget what they wanted for themselves, causing them to overachieve and doing so at their own emotional and physical expense. On the other extreme, they may stop trying altogether. The notion of trying and possibly failing would be too risky for them, so they stop making an effort. They avoid activities that can provoke anxiety and stay away from applying for new jobs or career changes, dating, or speaking in public. When women as young girls are constantly told they are dumb, stupid, not good enough, and daydreaming too much, they tend to get into a vicious circle of a negative thought pattern. They eventually start believing what they are told. Girls with undiagnosed ADHD tend to receive much more criticism in their childhood than neurotypical girls. Hearing these adjectives too many times may cause you to clip your proverbial wings. This may manifest as fear of going forward in careers or making life-changing decisions later on.

Women whose ADHD goes undiagnosed may also experience emotional dysregulation. This may manifest itself in both sexes and in different ways. One way is getting easily irritated and having a minuscule emotional threshold. Anything can set them off, and they get upset with the smallest of things. Certain information may rub them the wrong way. Most women with ADHD may also be introverts, leaving them to feel trapped by the circumstances that they are in and bottle up their emotions. They would often feel they are invisible to others. Although they might commit to something they love or enjoy doing, that feeling at the back of their mind will still lure them into perceiving themselves as losers and good-for-nothing. Keep in mind, these young women would have been called names throughout their childhood because their symptoms and behaviors were misconceived.

Women with undiagnosed ADHD can often experience executive dysfunction. Executive function is a set of skills used to perform tasks such as paying attention, remembering information, and multitasking. Neurotypical individuals use these skills to plan, organize, pay attention, and manage their time effectively. These skills start developing from the ripe age of two and continue to fully evolve till the age of thirty. These skills are important in daily life and at the workplace. Executive dysfunction will make it harder for the individual to follow through on plans, remember things, abide by complex or detailed instructions, and execute a project or a task they have been assigned. Women with ADHD who also have executive dysfunction may misplace things, struggle with their time management, be unable or struggle to organize schedules and sticking to them, struggle with dealing with setbacks and frustration, and be unable to self-monitor emotions or behavior. This weakness in your brain's self-management system means that your day-to-day tasks will be affected. This will mean that errands or things around the house may not get done as often as they should or sometimes not at all. It can sometimes be the case that important things one needs to prioritize will often get put aside for much less important things. The latter might be something the sufferer finds much more fun and engaging, consequently resulting in the release of dopamine in the brain. Dopamine is a chemical produced by the body and used by your nervous system. Dopamine plays a role in the way we feel, and it affects moods and feelings of motivation and rewards. Because it helps us feel pleasure, it helps us find things that are interesting to us. Dopamine plays an even bigger role in mental health. Lack of dopamine levels will cause a lack of motivation and desire. ADHD itself may be exacerbated by a shortage of dopamine levels.

Let's look into the "hyper-focus" aspect of ADHD. Women with undiagnosed ADHD may also experience hyper-focus and essentially fixate on things or activities they love. This fixation may go on for extended periods, even blocking other things. This can be a positive attribute of ADHD if you think of it as persistence in striving at a particular task to excel in it. The issue with hyper-focus is that people with ADHD do not concentrate on one thing at a time, kind of like neurotypical individuals would do for their hobbies, for example. The issue arises when they hyper-focus on many things, moving from one thing to the next, leaving a lot of unfinished projects that will often never get done. Alternatively, hyper-focusing on a single task and ignoring the rest of the things you should be paying attention to may also pose an issue. When women with ADHD fix their attention on one task, it does not necessarily mean that that task is important or is the actual task they should be devoting most of their energy and time to. For them, that is what interests them, and they become oblivious to the rest of their surroundings, all the while ignoring other responsibilities. If you fixate on video games or online shopping, then yes, it might pose an issue. This may result in a lack of productivity at work, failed relationships, or setbacks in education.

Undiagnosed women with the inattentive type of ADHD still experience hyperactivity, but not as you would imagine young boys to be, jumping off walls. They experience the same feeling bottled up inside, leaving their brains constantly going. This results in sleep disturbances, causing them to focus on subtle sounds around them, like that bird outside their window or the humming sound of the refrigerator. Adult women with ADHD may still face difficulty paying attention, be impulsive or feel restless. Daily tasks can be a challenge for women with

ADHD and hyperactivity. They may miss deadlines or forget meetings. They may struggle to wait in line or wait their turn. This may result in mood swings or occasional outbursts of anger. They may have a hot temper or low tolerance to frustration. They will overall have trouble coping with stress. On top of this, they will also have to deal with whatever emotions they have going on at that moment.

Teens with ADHD face a unique set of challenges. Academic and personal expectations escalate during these years. Around the same time, these children struggle with common teenage problems such as exploring sexuality, gaining individuality, dealing with social pressure, and the difficulties of driving.

In a nutshell, this can be described as feelings and emotions that never switch off, making you constantly distracted and unable to focus. This might contribute to not getting much done at the end of it all. Neurodiverse people will thrive in the right environment and when surrounded by the right support system. Taking entrepreneurs as an example, people with ADHD tend to be self-employed or entrepreneurs. Many adults with ADHD opt to be self-employed because they tend to be more creative and have an entrepreneurial spirit. Others may struggle with getting or holding a job. Being their own boss will give them a more flexible schedule and may allow them to delegate tasks they are not so good at completing themselves. Although self-employment or entrepreneurship will present its set of challenges, it may provide the right flexibility for women with ADHD. We will look more into job opportunities in a later chapter.

Chapter 6:
Gender Differences in ADHD: Why Women Struggle More

D iagnostic principles that have been based on studies in men and an inadequate understanding of symptoms in females means females experience different pathways than boys and men with ADHD. This discrepancy results in a lack of understanding for women with this condition. There is no male or female type of ADHD, although women tend to exhibit traits of one of the subgroups of ADHD more than the others, the inattentive type. The more science learns about ADHD and its differences in men and women, the lesser the gap in its diagnosis. The inattentive form of ADHD is most common in girls, and since it has more internalized symptoms, it often goes unnoticed. Science and research have a lot of information on ADHD and its symptoms; however, this information is more based on boys than girls. Because there is ample information about the topic, it often gives us the notion of knowing enough about it; however, it is not the case at all in women with ADHD. Unlike men, women tend to also get comorbid disorders that show up at the same time as ADHD. This will often divert clinicians from diagnosing ADHD itself. Comorbid disorders could be personality disorders, eating disorders, and substance use.

During puberty, girls will have an exacerbation of symptoms associated with ADHD because of the drop in hormone levels. They would have lower estrogen levels that will, in turn, trigger more irritability, mood disruption, sleep disturbances, and concentration issues. Young women with ADHD have lower levels of self-efficacy and poorly cope with general life situations. Whilst physical aggression and other externalized behaviors tend to be higher in men and boys, depression and anxiety are higher in girls. Men will show external frustration while women will direct their pain and anger inwards. Women with undiagnosed ADHD are at a higher risk of experiencing problems in school, social setups, and relationships than neurotypical girls. Men with ADHD would typically be more hypersensitive, are unable to concentrate, and tend to change jobs more frequently. Women with ADHD will note psychological distress, low self-esteem, and feelings of incapacity. Women with ADHD will likely face time-management challenges, disorganization, overwhelm, struggle with money management alongside a history of anxiety and depression. Women with ADHD tend to suffer from separation anxiety disorder, also known as SAD, while men will be more likely to have opposition- defiant disorder. SAD is a disorder characterized by anxiety where one experiences excessively concerning levels of separation from home or individuals with whom they hold a strong connection. This will have them feeling extremely sad and have difficulty focusing when away from the people they love or away from their comfortable environment. Opposition defiant disorder, also known as ODD, is more characterized by repeated patterns of irritability, anger, arguing, and maliciousness. People suffering from ODD easily and often lose their temper and are often resentful. They may refuse to comply with rules or obey authoritative bodies. The fact that women often experience SAD and men experience ODD is greatly influenced by gender roles and societal expectations.

While women with ADHD may experience some of the same symptoms experienced by their male counterparts, women still have to endeavor under the imposed burden and restrictions imposed on gender roles. They have to deal with fluctuating hormones, unlike men, resulting in a higher tendency to self-doubt and self-harm. Although at face value, women and men with ADHD may display similar symptoms, in the long-term, women will face conclusively different fallouts. As a practical example, if a female with ADHD is disorganized and forgetful to the point where if she forgets to pick up her children from school, she may be perceived as lacking motherly instincts and disregarding her duties as a mother. A man will be more accepted in society to be disorganized and forgetful primarily because women are "assigned" to be homemakers. They are the ones expected to set appointments, take care of the house chores and the children. If a mother is is late to her child's first school play, it may be easily mistaken for her disordered life. Women may still try hard to hide these flaws and may be afraid to ask for help. They will often end up doubting themselves and back off when their integrity is questioned.

Women might feel that fitting in and conforming is the road to acceptance. Women with ADHD are constantly facing unpredictable feelings and emotions. Already anxious, they conclude that they do not deserve a support system because they are their own support system or should be. Due to the societal roles imposed on them, women will often point fingers at themselves for being too distracted and unable to cope with the daily responsibilities. They might allow their flaws like lack of motivation and disorganization to define who they are. Because they often self-criticize, they usually expect to be criticized by others. When women with ADHD lack support from their family members, they often direct their frustrations into outbursts intended for their other halves or children. Following such episodes of outbursts, they often end up feeling demoralized and regretful. When their ADHD is left undiagnosed, they will not attribute these episodes to their condition but rather blame it on their damaged character.

Hormone levels in women drop during the premenstrual phase leading to more enhanced ADHD symptoms. Low estrogen levels can trigger more irritability. This can all affect their concentration and sleep patterns. These signs and symptoms are similar to those of premenstrual dysphoric disorder, also known as PMDD. PMDD causes severe irritability, depression, and anxiety around two weeks before their menstrual cycle. These symptoms may subside two or three days after the period starts. It is more likely for a woman to be diagnosed with PMDD than ADHD, as the underlying symptoms of these two conditions are very similar and sometimes interchangeable. Women with ADHD are more prone to have hormone-related disorders such as PMDD or post-partum depression, for example. When estrogen levels decrease during menopause, women experience heightened symptoms of ADHD. During menopause, a woman may already be experiencing sleep disturbances, age-related cognitive changes such as slow processing of information and memory changes, and confusion. This intensifies her ADHD symptoms during menopause.

Women with ADHD rely heavily on their intelligence to compensate for their flaws, all the while struggling to maintain focus. This makes them question their abilities overall. Succeeding can require bigger portions of their energy and time. They often compare themselves to others who always seem to achieve more than them effortlessly. They are forced to self-monitor continuously and strive for perfection. They can spend most of their time preparing obsessively, and if they overlook minor details, they beat themselves up, making themselves feel unworthy of love and compassion.

Undiagnosed ADHD may not only take an emotional toll but also a physical one. Women with ADHD tend to complain of nausea, headaches, have irregular eating patterns, and may have higher BMI, also known as body mass index. They are more prone to fall for compulsive shopping and gambling. Because women with undiagnosed ADHD may have experienced early physical or sexual abuse, they may also have post-traumatic stress disorder knowns as PTSD. A consolidation of these comorbid issues may create an even more complex picture for clinicians.

If ADHD is left untreated in girls, it will go on to affect them at a later stage in life. Women, as we know, would be given greater responsibilities as they grow older and get a career or form families. Their low self-esteem will not allow them to put their needs first. They may postpone their regular check-ups and try to function with low amounts of sleep. They often depend on medication to treat their anxiety, chronic pain, disruptive sleep patterns, and depression. They may also self-medicate with drugs or alcohol. Although women might seem less symptomatic as they grow older, it does not necessarily mean they are suffering less. They may distance themselves from others in the hope of masking their despair. As they might feel unworthy, they may accept to endure physical or emotional abuse in an unhealthy relationship. Enduring an abusive relationship coupled with impulsivity, they are more likely to resort to self-harm than men. Undiagnosed women with ADHD are at a higher risk of suicidal thoughts and attempts and are likely to die earlier than men of unnatural causes, such as accidents.

The disastrous combination of internalized symptoms, hormonal changes, and societal pressure creates a series of stressors exclusive to females with ADHD. Women with ADHD can perceive their negative experiences more agonizingly than men. They are more likely to struggle with low self-esteem than men and feel lucky if things turn out well for them instead of praising themselves for a job well done. If we take the experiences of men with ADHD as a standard, we will fail to understand women with ADHD and how to diagnose them altogether. It may be more helpful to equate women with ADHD to women who do not have the disorder because this analysis can be done based on one variable, the condition. If men and women with ADHD are compared, you are more likely to miss traits in women because, as already established, women's symptoms exhibit themselves differently than that of men's.

Chapter 7:
ADHD and Relationships

A DHD can be detrimental to relationships if both the sufferer and the partner are not appreciative and understanding of this condition. All the symptoms of ADHD like distraction, procrastination, forgetfulness, and fixation can cause havoc in the relationship, often leading to its termination. Symptoms of ADHD may cause frustration, anger, and hurt to both parties.

Because people with ADHD tend to suffer from executive dysfunction, they may often show up late for dates or meetings with their other half. This may come across as disrespectful to the other party and may be misinterpreted for lack of interest. People with ADHD tend to be forgetful and misplace things often, including personal belongings. If you text your partner, who suffers from ADHD, and do not hear back from them for a day or so, they probably forgot to respond to your text or call unintentionally, and they might have misplaced their phone. People with ADHD also suffer from sleep issues, so they might lack sleep or sleep too much. So, if you texted them to see where they wish to go for dinner and they are yet to reply, they could be napping. If you have ADHD and spend a big portion of your time looking for your wallet, keys, or phone, it is not because you are disorganized or a mess; it is probably because of your neurodiversity. The one suffering from ADHD may start avoiding their neurotypical partners as much as possible to avoid being criticized.

If your partner is the one suffering from ADHD, you may see them doing the same. Certain behaviors may not bother someone whilst dating, but in a long-term relationship, their actions will reflect their interest in the relationship and wherever it is headed. This can often lead to failed relationships and frequent break-ups. It is important to bear in mind that the behavior of an ADHD individual is not a reflection of how they feel about their other half or the relationship itself, but rather, symptoms of ADHD. Instead of blaming their partners for what seems to be the lack of skills, one should be more aware of their behavior and work on accepting the challenges someone with ADHD would experience.

Dating someone with ADHD can, in the beginning, be fun, instinctive, and exciting. For a long-term relationship to work out, there needs to be mutual understanding and willingness. Remind your partner that they should not take your behavior personally because you probably do not intend to act the way you do and that you are harmless. Your neurotypical partner can feel devalued when you space out during a conversation, remind them that it is not intentional. Missing important details or committing to plans you forget or cannot honor later will make your partner feel ignored but making them aware of you and your condition should get them to understand your good intentions.

Inattention caused by ADHD in a relationship does not only mean losing stuff or spacing out during a conversation, but it can also mean getting bored. Boredom may be far more damaging to a relationship than misplacing your stuff.

People with ADHD look for things that are of personal interest and are challenging to them. They engage in new things, and ideally, these new challenging things have deadlines. All these factors contribute to firing up the dopamine levels in the brain. At the beginning of a relationship, the first three factors would all be present, making a relationship a new and challenging commitment, which all started because of the interest you had in each other. At the start of the relationship, people with ADHD can barely think about anything else except for this new commitment. All the attention and energy are lavished on their partner. As time goes by, the relationship may not be as stimulating as it was in the beginning, and people with a neurodiverse brain will shift their focus to ways to keep having fun with the hope to fire up their dopamine levels again. By this time, the non-ADHD partner would have gotten used to all the care and attention they were receiving, and as you can imagine, it will not feel good to them when you pull away. They may take it personally and might think you do not love them anymore. Before you start shifting to other things that will give you that dopamine kick, neurodiverse brains will do their best to preserve the relationship because they got hooked on the exclusive attention they received in the beginning. They can pretend everything is perfect in a relationship, even when it is obvious it is not. They want to preserve what is making them feel so good. If and once they realize that the relationship is not perfect, they may want to change the other person to protect it. In some instances, if boredom takes over, the ADHD partner may also turn to cheating and hope they do not hurt their partner and at the same time keep up the relationship whilst getting the high they need. With cheating comes lying; neurotypical individuals may lie to the other half with the same intent to keep up the relationship and avoid hurting the other.

Because people with ADHD tend to hyper-focus on all things of interest, they may go too fast at the beginning and push the relationship too fast too soon. This will give them the thrill of something new in their lives. Both parties in the relationship will get stuck in this cycle and might be a little hard to avoid altogether. Honesty is the best policy here. You must be honest with yourself and others. You must be honest about your needs and wants, your views, and what you want out of this. Achieving this might be a struggle if there isn't effective communication. It must be understood that two weeks in the relationship will not give either of the partners enough information to determine whether they are the perfect match for each other. Two years down the line, the relationship will probably not be so exciting and euphoric as it was in the beginning. Nonetheless, it will be very hard to sustain the same excitement as two years prior. If you are in the relationship for the dopamine high, you need to understand that this will someday end, and the other person will still be there.

If you are honest with each other and know where you stand, it will become less challenging because, although you will have to work out solutions to make it work for both of you, you will be working towards previously discussed goals. You will only get involved with people that are interested in you and vice versa. With constructive and open communication, you will constantly reinvent yourselves and the relationship. This creates a deeper connection between the parties, making it even more interesting. If you feel emotionally charged at any given moment, it is best if you take a break and walk away. Come back only when you are ready to really listen to each other and work together to identify the root problem. It is important to not bottle up emotions but rather deal with them as they come. It is important to watch what you say, although this may be challenging if you are impulsive. Adding a little humor to the situation will lighten things up. Going in with the right mindset of listening to understand will completely reshape your perspective on issues.

This advice is for your partner: To help with communication in a relationship when one of the partners has ADHD, it will help if there are fixed times for discussions, so they are aware of the plans and are able to follow through a lot easier. It also helps to set up external reminders like whiteboards or sticky notes. Since people with ADHD get easily distracted, it is best if clutter is avoided around the house to help them stay focused. If you want to verify whether your partner with ADHD understood what you said, you can ask them to repeat the requests. Once this harmony is achieved, neurotypical brains can stop worrying about ending it, finding, or trying to save the relationship. This will enable people with ADHD to look for other things they can hyper-focus on other than the relationship and will be in it for their partner. Establishing the right support system in a relationship is essential to keep the relationship going. It is important to be compassionate and try to find the good in your partner.

It is understandable to mess up at times, and if both partners are fully invested and aware of each other, it will work out. One must work hard to prevent the relationship from becoming a co-dependent one, where only one partner is trying to make the relationship work. Make sure that duties and responsibilities are divided, and one party is not picking up too much slack for the other. It is understandable for tasks to be assigned to whoever does them best. People with ADHD may feel like they lack some skills and will feel more at ease to have certain tasks done by their other half. If the load is divided equally and one does not feel more invested than the other, it should work out just fine. Some of the simplest of tasks like chores can be difficult for people with ADHD to complete, not because they find them physically hard but because they are tedious duties that do not strike any interest in them. It will be very beneficial for the person with ADHD to received clear instructions regarding priorities and get help completing the most important tasks. Remember, it is very easy for neurodiverse brains to get side-tracked by the less important things if it is interesting to them. Hiring help at home or a professional organizer can help ease the load on the relationship. Most often than not, the issue with a relationship where one of the partners is neurodiverse is misunderstanding and misinterpreting actions and intents. Couple therapy can also be beneficial even though things might not seem to be going bad. It is suggested that this state is avoided altogether, and even if there are no serious or threatening issues you wish to address at any given time, therapy will help you learn effective communication.

Lastly, it is important to never look at the neurodiverse partner and see them as a burden or a duty, but rather think of it as having a partner who is trying to accommodate one's needs, but their condition gets in the way of that. There are ways of overcoming this, and working together is where it all starts.

Chapter 8:
ADHD and Motivation

Motivation is inconsistent in people with ADHD. When they focus their attention on certain tasks, they manage to complete them easily but struggle to find the spark to start others. From the neurotypical perspective, people who manage to focus on one task should be able to focus on every task in the same way. This can come across as a lack of willpower and just being lazy. This is not a willpower issue but a problem in the chemical dynamics of the brain. The process by which their perception and consciousness change towards things they find interesting is not voluntary. ADHDers can struggle with their working memory for prioritizing duties step by step. Emotions are a powerful and critical aspect of motivation. Emotions play an important role in executive functions like initiation, prioritization, maintaining or shifting interest, holding logic in memory, and picking tasks or avoiding them. The brain responds to the intensity of emotions relating to memories. Executive functions are not only driven by conscious feelings but also by unconscious ones. These unconscious emotions cause one to act inconsistently. Usually, this process leads to failure to complete tasks, disengage from actions altogether, or doubt if a task is completed. Someone with ADHD may want to complete the task and want to give it their full attention; however, they do not manage to act upon it. They will continue to procrastinate and put it off. ADHDers seek distraction and spend their time on less important things.

Individuals with ADHD have been shown to have consistently insufficient release and reloading of the neurotransmitter dopamine at synaptic junctions of neurons in the executive function networks. Stimulant medication may only work for tasks that the individual is interested in. If someone with ADHD, under stimulant medication, is presented with a task that interests them, then the stimulant medication will take hyper-focusing to another level during such tasks. This would usually be because that task has brought a positive feeling to the individual, or they recall positive memories when performing said task. Someone who has been postponing tasks till the very last minute, something people with ADHD tend to do, works better under pressure because they fear an unpleasant situation like missing a deadline. This fear increases dopamine release in the brain instantly and can help the individual maintain focus and interest to complete the task.

Working memory is another issue present in people with ADHD, and this is required to prioritize tasks one at a time according to their importance. People with larger working memory can deal with emotions, whether positive or negative ones. People with ADHD struggle to link memories to tasks abruptly and may find it difficult to see the complete picture. Think of someone watching a game through binoculars. They focus on the action and fail to see the rest of the court and what is happening around it.

Parents with ADHD, for instance, may struggle to express anger or scold their kids without making a scene. When neurotypical parents feel rage is taking over their emotions, their working memory helps them to remember their love towards their kids, and they calmly tell their kids what they did was wrong.

These are ways people with ADHD can overcome their lack of motivation:

1. Celebrate small milestones. Try incorporating things that can feel rewarding during the day and give this priority. Make sure you do not just focus on work but also include creative tasks that you enjoy doing. You can make a small list of things you can do to celebrate when you have completed small tasks. Set rewards for when the small tasks are completed so you can have something to look forward to. Try sticking to small but frequent rewards rather than far-fetched ones; otherwise, you can get discouraged.

2. Remove uncertainty in your life. Try conquering your lack of motivation by sounding more certain in your decisions. Avoiding using 'should' instead of 'must' for things you know you have to do. Try finding the little positive things in the tasks you avoid doing. Although you hate doing the laundry, try keeping in mind that once your laundry baskets are empty and your clothes are organized, you feel accomplished and motivated, and you can't get this feeling unless you do the laundry.

3. Be creative. If you have been assigned a task or know you have to complete a chore, try to think of creative ways you can complete this task, and if someone else can do it better than you do not be afraid to assign it to them, in exchange for a task you like doing. If you do not have this luxury, you can always outsource your tasks, like getting a housekeeper every so often

to help you clean the house if you dread doing it alone or avoid it altogether.

4. Customizing tasks according to your interests. If you must complete this task and no one else can do it on your behalf, try to change the process according to your needs. You do not have to complete a task according to what everyone else does or using their methods. These will probably not work for you. If you struggle to complete your grocery list because you get distracted during peak hours, try going later during the day or meet up with a friend and turn this into an outing.

5. Make the process exciting for you. Make sure you treat yourself when you complete the task and try setting a timer if you work better under pressure. If the task feels overwhelming, try planning ahead of time so you can divide it into different milestones. You can find it easier to complete simpler tasks and can reward yourself as you go along.

Make sure you identify what excites and recharges you; otherwise, you will not know what tasks you are willing to complete and those you dread. If you have set limitations for yourself because of past failures, make sure you identify these instances and, if needed, speak to a therapist. Ensure you always know who the second-best option is to complete the task on your behalf and know you need to be willing to exchange tasks. Try recalling a time when you managed to complete the task and identify the differences between then and now. Try bringing back some of those elements into the present situation to help you complete the task or at least find the motivation to start. Do not be afraid to divide the tasks into smaller ones and find whatever works for you. Identify your strengths and let go of negative self-talk that hinders your ability to complete tasks and motivate yourself. Identify why that task is meaningful or important for you. This way you will be encouraged to see the bigger picture. Find the best time to start the task, ideally not too close to its deadline. Identify what support you have or need to complete this task, and if those around you are aware of your ADHD and can assist or help facilitate the process for you, do not hesitate to ask for their help. Identify the obstacles you have and try to eliminate most of them. Finally, make sure you find creative ways to complete your goals because otherwise, the process of completing them will be a treacherous one.

Adults and children with ADHD are often stereotyped as unmotivated, lazy, or even apathetic. These derogatory labels are both unjust and harmful. Understanding these impairments is essential to address widespread misconceptions about ADHD. Neurodiverse brains can describe their lack of motivation to complete or initiate a task as almost paralysis. This feeling of helplessness can easily lead to feelings of overwhelm, procrastination, and avoidance, which can lead to productivity issues. Neurotypical brains can often become frustrated and confused by people with ADHD who are unable to perform well when a task is tedious and monotonous. It is not a matter of not knowing what to do, but people with ADHD can start the task and struggle to complete it. If a task is repetitive, it can make someone with ADHD feel frustrated and demotivated.

If the people around you struggle to understand your motivation and your lack of it in different scenarios, try explaining to them that you experience a disconnect between your intentions and goals. If they think this can simply be hurdled by inspiration, motivation, and self-discipline, explain that you may have had instances where you completed this task without issue, but the reason you are struggling now is not laziness. Neurotypical brains can struggle with lengthy, repetitive, and boring tasks. Urgent and novel things will strike a motivation in you like no other, especially if it interests you. Working under pressure or with urgency can give you a dopamine kick and get you working on your task. Stimulating and engaging activities are things you know you can complete if you have ADHD. Seeking stimulation via medication or exercise is not a luxury for people with ADHD but a necessity. If your superiors at work know you have ADHD, you may ask them to create different deadlines before the major one to help you submit minor parts of the project and to help you avoid procrastinating till the very last minute to complete a project. If you are in school, try asking your teacher for mini-deadlines for drafts of your assignment or otherwise find a close friend who can keep you accountable. Having someone to answer to can encourage you to keep up with deadlines. If you often feel ashamed to have people over because your house is always a mess, try inviting your friends over, so you are bound to clear the clutter and organize your space for when guests come over.

If you have taken up hobbies, you must understand that whatever feels interesting now may no longer be in a few months, and that is fine. You may have a list of things you enjoy doing, and if you are fed up with some, you can have a list to chose from but know you can always go back to playing that old guitar of yours whenever the motivation is rekindled.

Chapter 9:
ADHD and Social Skills

I mpulsive, disorganized, violent, overly sensitive, intense, emotional, or destructive actions are common perceptions in people with ADHD. Their relationships with others in their social world, parents, siblings, teachers, colleagues, co-workers, and spouses or partners, are often marred by confusion and miscommunication. The ability to self-regulate one's behavior and reactions toward others is impaired in people with ADHD. Relationships may become unnecessarily strained and unstable because of this. As a result of their inattention, impulsivity, and hyperactivity, people with ADHD often face social challenges, social rejection, and interpersonal relationship issues. Emotional pain and suffering are caused by such negative interpersonal outcomes. They tend to play a role in the development of comorbid mood and anxiety disorders as well.

To interact viably with others, an individual should be mindful and ready to control indiscreet practices. Grown-ups with ADHD are frequently unmindful and careless and regularly need reminders to control their behavior. Since ADHD is an "undetectable incapacity," often unnoticed by the individuals who might be new to the problem, socially unseemly practices that are the side effects of ADHD are frequently attributed to different causes. That is, individuals regularly see these practices and the person who submits them as inconsiderate, conceited, untrustworthy, apathetic, uncouth, and many other adverse character attributes. Over time, such negative marks lead to social dismissal of the person with ADHD. Social dismissal causes enthusiastic torment in the existence of many youngsters and grown-ups who have ADHD and can cause destruction and lower confidence levels for the duration of their life. In a relationship, improper social conduct may outrage the companion without ADHD, who may in the long run "wear out" and abandon the relationship or marriage. Educating people with ADHD, significant others, and their companions about ADHD and how it influences their social abilities and relational practices can help mitigate a large part of the contention and fault. Simultaneously, the person with ADHD needs to learn procedures to become as capable and conceivable in a social environment, so effort needs to go both ways. With appropriate appraisal, treatment, and training, people with ADHD can figure out how to communicate with others viably such that it improves their public image.

Observing people, copying their actions, practicing, and receiving input are common ways to learn social skills. They may grasp what is proper yet come up short in general on social expectations. Shockingly, as grown-ups, they regularly acknowledge "something" is missing yet are never fully sure what that "something" might be. Social acknowledgment can be seen as going up or down. People who show proper social abilities are compensated with more acknowledgment from those they socialize with and are encouraged to utilize their friendly abilities. For those with ADHD, the winding regularly goes the other way. Their absence of social abilities prompts peer dismissal, limiting the freedom to master social skills, which prompts more dismissal, and the cycle goes on. Social discipline incorporates dismissal, evasion, and other more obvious methods for displaying one's objection towards someone else. Note that individuals do not frequently tell the offender the reason for the social infringement.

54

Calling attention to a social mistake is frequently considered socially unacceptable. Hence, individuals are almost always left all alone to attempt to improve their social abilities without seeing precisely what aspects need improvement because there is no feedback from others.

Try to be more observant of your environment and mindful of other people's actions. Make sure you notice other's body language, tone of voice, and behavior. Do not avoid eye contact but rather maintain it. Give enough importance to other people's choice of words as that can translate into what they want to say. For example, if they say they would love to do something, they probably want to do it. Be attentive to actions because they speak louder than words. If they say one thing and do another, believe their actions because they are more reliable and reveal their true self. If you have someone around you that you trust, and they know about your ADHD, try telling them about your perceptions and see if you are on the same page. Do not be afraid to ask for various perspectives from different people. Someone with ADHD can be engaged in a conversation and miss the main point of the conversation. If they ask again to verify or gather what they have missed, they are often perceived as inattentive and missing out on details intentionally, when this is not the case. Repeating information can be frustrating for the other party. People with ADHD can struggle with translating communication adequately enough for them to understand it, let alone reading between the lines. This can pose an issue because what is said is not always what is meant, so ADHDers can often miss the message implied by the other parties.

Impulsivity adversely influences social connections since others may credit imprudent words or activities to the absence of really focusing or respecting others. The inability to pause and think first regularly destroys social results. Rushed activities can likewise challenge people with ADHD and have them acting before thoroughly considering their conduct. Settling on choices dependent on an "at the time" attitude regularly prompts a helpless dynamic. Those with ADHD regularly end up baited off task by something seriously welcoming. Indiscreet shifting from one task can incorporate taking crazy risks, inability to read or plan for school or business-related activities, stopping occupations, settling on choices to move, monetary overspending, and surprisingly forceful activities, like hitting others or tossing things. Quick and over-the-top discourse can likewise be an indication of impulsivity. The quick-fire discourse of a person with ADHD pretty much rules out other people who should participate in the discussion. Physical hyperactivity can make it difficult to participate in recreational activities. Others can view a person's inability to sit still and focus during concerts, religious activities, lectures, or even holidays as a lack of care or consideration on the part of the person with ADHD. Furthermore, the inability to be attentive makes others feel unattended.

During an ADHD assessment, the physician takes into consideration the individual's social skills and can ask for a report from the ADHDer and their spouses or partners for confirmation.

These reports can often include the following incidents:

- Paying attention when spoken to is difficult and often misses vital details.

- Appears to be unconcerned with others.

- Taking turns in conversation is difficult.

- Tendency to interrupt frequently.

- Having trouble completing activities or duties.

- Inability to use correct etiquette.

- Misses verbal cues.

- Living an unorganized way of life.

- Shares information inappropriately.

- Find noises or vibrations others can easily shut out distracting.

- Immediately shutting down when feeling swamped or frustrated.

- Thoughts that are disorganized.

- Abruptly ending a discussion.

- Have trouble keeping friends or maintaining relationships.

- Going off-topic during conversations and getting distracted by unrelated thoughts.

- Being unreliable because you give off the vibe of someone who can be counted on, but you fail to meet deadlines.

- Overreacting, lashing out, or having meltdowns when it is not appropriate.

Social skills can be worked upon, and once the flaws are identified, it is important to speak to an ADHD coach or a therapist who can help you better these skills. Medication usually helps with certain impulsive actions and hyperactivity because it allows for more concentration and self-control; however, medications alone cannot provide the sufficient help needed to gain the required skills for socializing. Therapy can often include role-play, modeling, feedback, and instructions. There are also ways to improve social skills through changes you apply yourself. Start by gaining knowledge on social skills and identify areas that need improvement. Apply a positive attitude and make sure you are open to growth. Make sure you are open to feedback and take this constructively and not personally. Once you identify your flaws, make sure you take one skill at a time and improve on it as you go. Make sure you master one skill before you move on to the next one. If you are struggling with gathering all the important information in a conversation, try to ask for a repetition of what was said to clarify and make sure you understood everything said without leaving out any major details. If you look up to someone around you and feel like their skills are way developed than yours, use them as a model. Once you gain these skills, try practicing them via role-playing. Allow the person you are practicing with to provide you with feedback. If you cannot do role-play, you can also try visualizing circumstances under which you can utilize these skills. Try running it through your mind and practice it as much as possible. Make sure that visualizations are realistic and practice the skill in situations and with people you are likely to need it. ADHDers who lack social skills may use prompts to help them stay on track. If you are often fidgety and talk a lot, try setting reminders on your watch every five minutes. People who are honest, loyal, understanding, trustworthy, considerate, and reliable are more likely to have social relationships. Try developing these skills, and you will be more likely to create and maintain healthy relationships.

With the help of combined treatment like therapy and medication, if you are already on any, you can learn to stop before you speak your mind and filter any inappropriate information you are about to give to others. Making those around you aware of your ADHD wherever possible can help them understand your intentions if you slip up and avoid misunderstanding you. If you feel like you never fit in or struggle to make new friends, it is because your social skills are lacking due to your ADHD.

Although you might feel anxious attending social events, try to go with someone you feel comfortable with and can keep you company while there. If you feel like you are not invited to parties or events often, try inviting people over instead. Try engaging in activities one at a time and try sticking to things you know you can handle, like meeting for walks in the parks, to begin with rather than skipping to watching movies with friends immediately. If the first wedding you've been invited to is coming up next month, try asking someone who has the experience to walk you through it. If you are unsure of the social etiquette, dress code, and who to take as a guest, ask someone you trust for honest feedback. The more you practice, the more comfortable you will be. Accept feedback from others and make sure you do not take it the wrong way but use it to improve. Take examples from people who you know and feel are good at socializing. You do not have to look at them and feel bad about yourself but rather be opportunistic and allow yourself to grow. Do not take advice from people who strive to be people pleasers or do things to be liked by others; that is not the right way to improve your social skills. If you feel anxious around certain people or when attending events, it means you are not ready for that yet. It is acceptable to refuse to attend such activities if, besides hindering your learning, it also makes you anxious and uncomfortable.

While ADHD can make social interactions more difficult, there is knowledge and services available to help you develop your social skills. Get advice from books, therapy, or coaching, and most importantly, make and sustain social ties. You do not need a lot of friends to improve your skills. A small circle of reliable and honest friends is all you need.

Chapter 10:
ADHD and Social Anxiety

S ocial anxiety disorder, also known as SAD, is one of the most common anxiety disorders that can coexist with ADHD. In one or more social contexts, social anxiety is correlated with a distinct fear of possibly devastating attention and judgment from others. Worries about embarrassment and rejection are common in people with social anxiety, and they can last for six months or longer. Worrying about being judged negatively by others can limit involvement in events, interests, and relationships; it can also make it difficult to form new relationships. It is crucial to understand the nuances between the two conditions when it comes to managing and treating them. Although experts are unsure why ADHD and SAD always coexist, some believe that the same factors that trigger ADHD, like genetics, environmental contaminants, or premature birth, may often exacerbate anxiety disorders. Others agree that the signs of ADHD, in and of themselves, lead to anxiety. Inattention, hyperactivity, and impulsivity are common symptoms of ADHD, and they place a person at risk of being ridiculed, mocked, or otherwise socially rejected. Fearing more rejection, many people withdraw into themselves, avoiding any potentially threatening social situations. At first glance, ADHD and SAD may seem the same. If you suffer from SAD, you are constantly concerned about being viewed negatively by others. You might find it difficult to eat or speak in public or use public restrooms. It might be difficult for you to attend social gatherings. You may be aware that your fear is unfounded, but you feel helpless to change it, as with other anxiety disorders.

The following are some symptoms where ADHD and SAD overlap:

Struggle to socialize- Because people with SAD fear rejection, they struggle to socialize. Likewise, people with ADHD can also struggle to read between the lines and have low control over their impulses resulting in a lack of maintained social relations.

Inattentive- People with ADHD can often come across as inattentive, and that is because their brain affects their focus. People with SAD can also seem inattentive, and that is because their brain is taken over by worrisome thoughts.

Struggle completing tasks- People with SAD often struggle to complete tasks, and those with ADHD also find difficulty sticking to deadlines or plans as they should.

Some of the symptoms of SAD can be misinterpreted, and people with ADHD may not get diagnosed with SAD because of this. If you have both SAD and ADHD, your doctor can properly evaluate your symptoms and deduce which ones are causing you the most impairment. If possible, the doctor can treat these two conditions together or otherwise opt to treat the one that is interfering with your life the most. If ADHD is what is causing your SAD symptoms, then managing your ADHD can help solve both issues. Medications that can help both SAD and ADHD can be either non-stimulant medication or stimulant ones. Stimulant medication increases the levels of certain brain chemicals, such as dopamine and norepinephrine. They allow nerves in your brain to communicate with one another. They are also generated in reaction to pleasurable experiences. Non-stimulant medication increases the level of norepinephrine, a critical brain chemical. This tends to increase attention span while decreasing impulsive behavior and hyperactivity. Because medication will not cure all problems, therapy can also be a great solution for treating SAD and managing ADHD. Many of the underlying issues of both ADHD and SAD, as well as the complex symptoms that overlap between them, can be addressed through cognitive behavioral therapy (CBT). CBT aims to teach people with SAD strategies and practice controlling their anxiety. Exposure therapy, a form of CBT most often used to treat SAD, is a method in which you and your therapist work together to gradually introduce you to anxiety-provoking scenarios so that you can build healthier coping strategies and eradicate associated fear over time. You can learn and practice social skills and other aspects of CBT and learn relaxation techniques.

SAD is not the same as shyness. Shyness is regarded as a personality characteristic. When confronted with a social or interpersonal situation, shy people feel nervous or anxious, but they understand that being shy is a part of who they are, much like bubbly people. Social anxiety sufferers can be reserved or extroverts, but they see SAD as a negative trait and are often critical of themselves for feeling this way. The signs of SAD are:

- Self-consciousness in front of others.

- Extreme fear of being judged.

- Feel anxious and worry for days before a social event.

- Feel intensely uncomfortable in social situations.

- Avoid social situations altogether.

- Struggle to make or keep friends.

- Experience panic attacks, including shaking, sweaty palms, nausea in social situations.

- Struggle to start a conversation or talk to others.

- Feel uncomfortable talking to people unless it is immediate friends or family members.

- Feel afraid that people will negatively judge you.

Not everyone experiences all of these symptoms. Some individuals may only show symptoms in a specific situation, while others may show symptoms in a variety of social circumstances. Although some people with SAD choose to remain in the shadows, others are outgoing in places where they are not required to perform the behavior that causes them problems. Only when an individual's causes are triggered do symptoms of social anxiety disorder appear. SAD can make it difficult to make new friends and engage in social activities. Your fear of answering questions or speaking in class can cause problems in school. If you must be able to speak publicly and present to the rest of your team at work if you are given a promotion, you might decide not to go in for the promotion. If you are required to deal with customers, especially in unpleasant situations, you may struggle to complete your duties at work. Teens who suffer from social anxiety are often depressed. According to some studies, people with SAD are more likely to also have dysthymia, which is a severe depressive disorder, or another mood condition. Early intervention can help to minimize the risk of depression and other coexisting conditions. An over-reaction to a stimulus or a circumstance is one tell-tale sign of social anxiety. For example, a person can be so sure that everyone is staring at them, even if no one is paying attention while waiting in line for a muffin and coffee that they refuse to stay and place their order. Many people who suffer from social anxiety are aware that their acts are illogical, but they are powerless to alter them. They feel bad for themselves and wish they could be someone else. However, with the right help, you can successfully handle social anxiety if you want to improve.

Try these simple steps to start reducing your social anxiety:

Focus on one thing- Begin by looking for quick wins to boost your confidence in yourself and self-esteem. What is the one thing you wish you could change that is causing you the most difficulty right now? Focus on this target repeatedly to summon the will to confront what worries you. Find someone to help you in this process. You'll need someone to hold you accountable, such as a sibling, a relative, a psychiatrist, or a mentor.

Start light- Start small to avoid being discouraged at first. Before taking on a larger mission, master a transition that is within your grasp. For example, if you are shy about meeting new people but want to make new friends, expecting to make 10 friends on your first try might be asking too much of yourself. Instead, consider the first, very small move you might take: ask someone you do not know a question.

Be compassionate with yourself- People who have ADHD and social anxiety tend to be very critical of themselves. For years, you have heard cynical stories about how you have missed the mark and what you should do differently. You continue to unwittingly follow this dialogue over time. When it comes to dealing with social anxiety, pessimistic self-talk is the worst enemy. Begin by thinking about something inspirational you might say to yourself, "I am smarter than I thought," for example. Write it on Post-It notes and place them at vantage points within your surrounding. This may sound corny, but you need to know what to say to the cynical voice when it tells you that you can't take a risk to try anything new. Consider keeping a written diary in which you record one daily achievement about your challenge. Go back to it whenever you feel down because you failed one task, and it also helps to keep yourself accountable and on track.

Be mindful- When you are having a panic attack or are caught up in a guilt trip as a result of social anxiety, try to become more conscious of your physical body and your breathing. This is your exit ticket from the spiral. When people are nervous, their breathing picks up as adrenaline takes over. This is our fight or flight reaction at work. In these situations, you must ground yourself and slow down your breathing. Try putting one hand on your shoulders and the other on your stomach. Breathe into both hands, feeling their weight, and pretend that you are breathing in a soothing color with each breath. Do this for a few minutes. Alternate nostril breathing from yoga can also be used for five rounds. You can feel uncomfortable and insecure when you work to alleviate your anxiety. Those are indications that you're on the right track.

Talk to someone every day- You must exercise your social skills, even though you do not want to. Combat your natural proclivity toward loneliness by engaging in a 3 to 5-minute interaction with someone outside your home at least three days per week. It can be done via Zoom or FaceTime, over the internet, or in person, but you must make real-time contact with someone who cannot be reached via text messaging or social media. Make a list of people you call: distant or near relatives, cousins, siblings who have passed on, grandparents, and so on. You cannot enhance your ability to communicate with others or read their emotional state by email, which is precisely the talent you need to develop. If you are unsure what to say, prepare any questions ahead of time or ask your accountability partner for assistance and practice. Having a list of people you know you can go to practice and enhance your skill is much easier than having to think at the top of your head because you are less likely to be encouraged and talk to strangers or to people you do not feel comfortable with.

Anxiety is a formidable opponent that tries to keep you disarmed, so it takes bravery and maturity to face it. To effectively address social anxiety, you must first set a fair and achievable target and be prepared to feel some discomfort along the way. That is how you can learn and develop the skills you need to gain the social trust and relationships you desire. You cannot be able to get rid of all the social anxiety at once. It serves a useful but unwanted purpose: it protects you from pain. Although unintentionally, you may fall short because fear is a normal part of being human. The aim is to lessen its impact on your life, which is more practical.

Chapter 11:
ADHD and Sleep Problems

O ver half of adults with ADHD report going to bed late and waking up late. They also confess to having trouble with feeling tired after a night of sleep during the day if they do not wake up late. They rarely manage to fall asleep effortlessly or wake up feeling good in the morning.

The physical and mental restlessness in adults with ADHD disrupts a person's sleep, leaving them with exhaustion. The reason why there was never a direct link between sleep issues and ADHD is that this was not strongly evident in kids with ADHD but became more consistently present in adults with ADHD. To date, sleep disturbances are considered as coexisting issues of ADHD, and medication used to treat ADHD may have been accused of interfering with healthy sleeping patterns in people with ADHD. Sufferers call this perverse sleep, which pretty much works in reverse; they are awake when they want to be asleep and fall asleep when they want to stay awake. This is also known as delayed sleep phase syndrome. People with ADHD tend to have trouble with their circadian rhythm, sometimes also referred to as the internal clock. This regulates sleep and wake patterns. Melatonin production is affected by this rhythm. Melatonin is a chemical that makes us feel sleepy. This naturally occurring peptide in the body is produced following the rising and setting of the sun, supposedly. The internal clocks in neurodiverse individuals still produce melatonin, but not at the right time. This could be because circadian rhythms are off naturally or because a certain behavior creates or reinforces this disrupted rhythm. Your internal clock can be reset either by medications, which your doctor will prescribe as they deem fit or by controlling light exposure. To reset one's internal clock, one might need to get exposed to sunlight in the morning and avoid it late at night. There are alarm clocks that are stimulated by sunlight that can help one wake up when they need to. Once successful, this will help set one's internal clock and may also help with time management. People with ADHD tend to have a false sense of time, and this also contributes to them being late a lot of times.

A lot of people with ADHD report restlessness, specifically at night. They describe it as their mind racing as soon as they decide to fall asleep, leaving them unable to sleep at night. They might also describe themselves as night-owls and tend to work better at night. They would not be morning persons, and completing the simplest of tasks in the morning can prove to be extremely challenging. Some also report taking over an hour trying to fall asleep at night. When people with ADHD manage to fall asleep, they often toss and turn a lot and are very sensitive to noises around them. They wake up to the slightest sound, which mostly reduces the hours and quality of sleep, having them wake up in the morning as tired as they went to bed the night before. People with ADHD often wake up multiple times during the night, and when they manage to get into a deep sleep, they find it very hard to wake up in the morning. They will eventually wake but do so groggily and may need a huge cup of coffee to kickstart the brain.

People with ADHD will disengage if something does not interest them. This may cause them to feel drowsy and may get them to fall asleep, wherever they are; this might be in a meeting or in class. This can often be mistaken for EEG negative narcolepsy. EEG stands for electroencephalography, and it is a test used to detect electrical activity in the brain using electrodes attached to the scalp. EEG is a test used to diagnose various brain disorders, including epilepsy, encephalitis, sleep, and other disorders. It is also used to diagnose narcolepsy, which is a neurological condition that causes excessive daytime sleepiness. People with ADHD who fall asleep during the day may be misdiagnosed with narcolepsy instead.

It is suggested that improved sleep hygiene is applied. This will foster and initiate the sleep process and hopefully maintain it. Sleep hygiene can vary according to the individual. Ideally, and as a standard, the bed should be kept as a place for sleep and intimate action, not to argue or to work. You must have a set bedtime routine, and many phone applications can help you do this. It would be beneficial to consider avoiding naps during the day. If you require specific sounds or music, make sure you have it set up by the time you go to bed. Warm showers or baths can help you get sleepier. If some sounds bother you at night or hinder your sleep, try your best to eliminate them, and try wearing earplugs to block out noise. If you want to try and go to sleep, try getting into bed to begin with. Avoid drinking coffee late at night because we all know caffeine will keep you awake and because it is a diuretic, it will also wake you up several times during the night for multiple visits to the bathroom. Ideally, consumption of any liquids is minimalized closer to bedtime, and gadgets like your tablet or laptop should be put down 2 to 3 hours before bedtime as the blue light they emit will hinder the production of melatonin, making you unable to fall asleep. If you must work late at night, try using a blue light filter to avoid disrupting your sleep. Some spectacles can come with this filter even if you do not have to wear prescription glasses, so the lens serves purely as a blue light filter. Certain foods are also said to help and promote sleep, such as kiwis, nuts, tart cherries juice, and grapes. Valerian and chamomile teas also help. Meditating 10 to 15 minutes before bedtime can help you relax.

There are plenty of things one can do to promote a healthier sleeping pattern, but it starts by giving your symptoms the diagnosis and importance they deserve. If your ADHD is overlooked, you will, in return, receive inadequate treatment.

Chapter 12:
ADHD and Emotional Dysregulation

I f you have ADHD and find yourself on an emotional rollercoaster, it is probably caused by your emotional dysregulation. This is a big part of how ADHD affects the lives of neurodiverse individuals. Some doctors do not consider emotional dysregulation as one of the symptoms of ADHD because the literature they use to help identify people with ADHD does not list emotional dysregulation as being part of them. Researchers wanted to measure results that could be assessed in a laboratory, but emotions are a bit hard to compute like that. Research is, all the time, evolving, and there is an understanding of emotional dysregulation and its prominence in ADHD.

People with ADHD feel and experience the same emotions as any neurotypical individual; the issue is regulating those emotions. Regulation will give you the ability to calm down and make the right choices when something gets to you. The process of regulating emotions is a process that tends to rely on characteristics an ADHD brain struggle with or lack. This process starts with inhibition. This means you do not impulsively react to an emotion. Regular people would not struggle to achieve this, but people with ADHD can find this to be a hard task when you are naturally impulsive already. Some say that the more generally impulsive one is, the more likely they are to be emotionally impulsive as well. Because of impulsivity, people with ADHD may not even surpass this step as they would spontaneously react to their emotions without controlling them. The next step of the process is self-soothing, which is the ability to calm down that initial emotion. Self-soothing methods may work for some, but they may not always be healthy choices. Consequently, one would need to refocus one's attention and energy towards regulation and not on negative thoughts or emotions. Lastly, one would need to act in line with their goals. It might not be easy for people with ADHD to go on with this last step because they must put in a lot of thought to consider their goals: what the other person said, what they want to say, what happened the last time something like this happened and analyze all the variables in that situation to try predicting the different possible outcomes based on this response and choose the best outcome. For someone with ADHD doing all this can be very challenging because of their limited working memory. This can be troubling in a school or work setup. This process happens with all emotions, from sadness to fear and excitement.

Emotional dysregulation can get in the way of one's goals and may make someone with ADHD not so fun to be around in certain situations if, for example, those around them do not understand their condition and their intentions. Emotional dysregulation will not always exhibit itself in the same way in different situations. It might help to keep track of your emotions and jot down how you feel in certain situations. This can help you identify your bad habits, and by being more aware of them, you can learn to avoid getting into these habits in the first place. In this way, you can understand better when your emotions are getting you in trouble or hindering your goals. Awareness is also where to start. Being aware of your emotions will help you slow down your emotional reactions leaving time for you to think and decide how you want to respond instead of reacting impulsively. This is also called mindfulness and is a method of meditation. This will make you more aware of your thoughts and interpreting them without judgment. You must be curious to explore ways to deal with these emotions to the best of your abilities. This will help to reduce stress overall.

Not everyone suffering from ADHD will experience emotional dysregulation, but those who do will often describe themselves as very emotional. Borderline personality disorder or mood disorder can also have emotional dysregulation as a symptom. This is also why people with ADHD, specifically women, may get misdiagnosed. People with emotional dysregulation can be sensitive to criticism, have perceived rejections, and be overly sensitive to teasing. They would often find it hard to brush of teasing comments from those around them and would take it very seriously. Emotional responses in people with emotional dysregulation are often displayed as emotional responses at a higher magnitude than those without this issue. It would be beneficial to let the people around you know what you are overly sensitive about and the jokes or teasing comments you would not tolerate. Those that care and understand you will do their best to avoid passing comments on things they know will upset you. People with emotional dysregulation often seem impatient, tense, and edgy. This would not necessarily mean someone finds it hard to sit still through a meeting or finds it hard to relax. It is more like extreme levels of frustration internally. For example, if technological devices, such as laptops or mobile phones, are faulty, you are likely to get frustrated because you need them to work. If something is not going to plan, it may also trigger emotional dysregulation, and one may find it hard to assess the situation in a practical way, detached from one's emotions.

Mood swings are also another symptom of emotional dysregulation. You may wake up in a negative mood only to end the day with a positive feeling. It might be difficult to deal with the negative moments in your life, but you must remember that nothing is permanent and that this too shall pass. You might feel negative about yourself because you had a target to reach, which you failed to do by mid-day but by the end of the day, something may happen that will turn your mood around. If you reflect on the past and realize that you've been in this situation before and recall how it ended, you will realize you are going to get through it. People with emotional dysregulation may also experience emotional outbursts. These reactions may seem. This may not always be the case for people with emotional dysregulation because some may bottle up their emotions leading to internal frustration rather than exerting their anger.

Lastly, people with emotional dysregulation can have a harder time going back to a neutral emotional baseline, and it will take them longer to get back to their calmer state. This can be highly impacted by the people you surround yourself with. If those around you have fluctuating emotions as well, it will leave you feeling uneasy, and because you are anxious and constantly on the lookout for when the other shoe will drop, you have a hard time feeling at ease around them. It is important who you surround yourself with because, from teasing and jokes to the positive or negative vibes they emit, it will all affect your emotions and how you feel towards those emotions. If you are surrounded by someone who makes you feel at ease, safe, and fully understands your flaws, they are more likely to understand your intentions and will be less likely to trigger or set your emotional dysregulation issue off even over frivolous things. On the other hand, if you are ringed by negative people whose emotions are even more alternating than yours, you are very likely to be anxious around them.

Emotional dysregulation can have its positive sides. People with ADHD can enjoy feeling strong emotions and are usually very sensitive to the emotions others around them experience, making them very empathetic. They easily get excited and are not able to hide that excitement. This makes people with ADHD very fun to be around. This makes them very interesting, passionate, and expressive people. Emotions are a way of communicating with ourselves and others too. They can also motivate new ventures, like when you are excited about an idea which you finally start working on and turn into a new project or business. A healthy diet with the right water intake coupled with the right amount of sleep will help make you feel less edgy and irritable. Physical activity will relieve stress, depression, anxiety, and symptoms of ADHD. Because physical activity increases endorphin release in the body, it will boost your overall mood. Regular short 10-minute walks can do magic for your mood. Meditation or yoga sessions can also help you relax. If you notice that caffeine or a high sugar intake makes you feel jittery or anxious, avoid them altogether. It is important to get help if you are experiencing emotional dysregulation because it often leads to problems in relationships and at work. It may lead to anxiety and depression. You may lean towards substance abuse to help cope with your emotions if this is left untreated. Cognitive behavior therapy can be very beneficial for people who experience emotional dysregulation as part of their ADHD and is usually given by therapists.

Chapter 13:
ADHD and Sexuality

A DHD in adults already impacts their lives, including difficulty maintaining stable relationships and fostering a poor self-image. Symptoms affecting sexuality can vary from person to person and may be hard to measure for this reason. Common ADHD symptoms can include emotional instability, depression, and anxiety. All of these can harm your sex drive. If you are constantly focusing your time and energy on staying organized, you will probably not have much energy left to get involved in sexual activities with your partner.

Two commonly reported symptoms of ADHD and sexuality are hypersexuality and hyposexuality. Although sexual dysfunction is not one of the diagnostic criteria for ADHD, it is still very much real. Hypersexuality refers to an uncommonly high sex drive. Sexual stimulation releases endorphins in the brain, giving a feeling of calmness and reducing restlessness— two very common feelings in people with ADHD. ADHD individuals are already probably very impulsive, and this may have them engage in risky sexual behavior. People with ADHD may also experience hyposexuality, where their sex drive drops. This may be due to the condition itself or caused by medications used to treat ADHD. The same issues people with ADHD face during normal day-to-day activities will also be faced during sex. They will have a hard time concentrating, may lose interest, and become distracted.

Women with ADHD may have trouble achieving orgasm because they either reach it too quickly or not at all despite lengthy stimulations.

People with ADHD may be hypersensitive, meaning they have extreme physical sensitivity. What may feel good to the non-ADHD partner may feel irritating to the ADHD sufferer. Odors, touch, and tastes often involved in sex may come across as nasty to someone with ADHD. Getting intimate in the first place can also be a challenge for people with ADHD because of their hyperactivity. They may struggle to relax enough to set the mood for sex. Neurodiverse brains are mostly always busy, and when their brain is focused on a million other things, it is very hard to transition into sex. ADHD individuals tend to get distracted during sex, particularly women, but even neurotypical brains do this. It is possible for people with ADHD to hold their focus throughout sex but initiating activity can be a challenge. ADHD brains tend to rate higher on sexual eagerness because they are more willing to try new things and may contribute to keeping things more exciting in the bedroom. This does not mean that all ADHD individuals experience sexuality the same way because everyone is different.

Surprisingly enough, ADHD and its effects on sexuality are not solely about sex itself but more about how ADHD is managed, either by ADHD brains or their partners. Whoever tries hard enough to manage their ADHD and makes sure their partners know they are trying will more likely experience intimacy when compared to those that do not put in the effort. Making the other party aware of your efforts is very important. It is easy to see that you are trying hard enough or putting in the effort because you are very aware of your actions. It will be a little harder knowing what your partner is doing because you cannot see it all. If awareness is not present, it will be easy to have one of the partners, usually the neurotypical one, feel like they work harder or put in more effort than their other half, usually the ADHDer. Putting in the effort the other party expects can be a good start, although the effort might not mean everything is as your partner expects it to be. They are more likely to appreciate your good intentions even though not everything is as they please. If they walk into the living room only to find a mess but know that it is you trying, they are more likely to feel happier towards you because they know you are doing the best you can. The neurotypical brain would feel that although their needs are not being met fully, there is an effort, and the intention is to try. If there is not enough communication and the non-ADHD partner does not recognize that their ADHD counterparts are putting in the effort, it may be demoralizing for the ADHDer. They may come across as careless when, in fact, they do care. If their effort goes unnoticed, they may be inclined to give up rather than try their best. ADHD needs to be managed by the partner suffering from it and by the neurodiverse partner.

Managing ADHD when it is not your own can come across as parenting your other half. This will often take a toll on your sex life because no one wants to get intimate with someone who they feel parental towards or who is being parental towards them. Think of it as teamwork, everyone needs to pool in their biggest strengths, and together, they will create something better for everyone. People with ADHD may fall into the trap of pleasing others and being co-dependent on their partners. If you are too co-dependent on your partner, it might limit your options. As a couple, you need to be able to speak your mind, and your partner needs to be there to hear it. If you are too co-dependent, you may settle to be treated less nicely than you should. This is because you might feel threatened or scared to push back and may settle for much less than you deserve. If people with ADHD feel they are not deserving of good treatment because they feel they are not doing well enough, they will be more at risk of becoming co-dependent on their partners. People with ADHD tend to be more forgetful, as I've stated previously, and because of this, they may punish themselves and be hesitant to ask for their needs to be met because they feel like they do not deserve it. If you take ADHD more seriously and put in the effort to manage the condition, you are more likely to remember your duties in the relationship and complete more and more of them. This will result in more harmony in the relationship where both parties feel their needs are being met or mostly met. With the right set-up, couples will want to have sex with each other. If the non-ADHD partner feels like their needs are being overlooked, they are more likely to complain about it as they would feel like they are putting in all the effort and they are alone. The ADHD partner will likely get defensive, discouraged and try minimizing the gravity of the situation. On the inside, the ADHD-partner would still feel that whatever it is that they are doing is not enough and is constantly failing. Non-ADHD partners may expect their ADHD partners to do things and complete tasks as a neurotypical brain would, but this is not possible for neurodiverse individuals. A partner that challenges you to bring out the best in yourself is the ideal partner. With that said, it is important that no one in the relationship feels like they are selling out their integrity and compromising more than they should. It should not be like you are doing too much for someone else but not enough for yourself. It is important to never get the feeling of someone doing too much and the other half not doing enough. A balance needs to be achieved so no one feels like they are either selfish or being used.

It can be ideal if, with compromise, couples chose to try new techniques to reduce the risk of boredom during sex. It is very important to be attentive and sensitive to the other person's feelings and goals. Any plans need to be approved by both partners. It is best to communicate and discuss how ADHD affects your intimacy. Partners need to be considerate to each other's needs and adjust accordingly. If perfumes or light bother the partner with ADHD, then agree to avoid these triggers altogether in the bedroom. Sex therapy or couple therapy can also be beneficial. Doing calming exercises before the act can help get you both in the mood, like yoga and meditation. Try getting rid of distractions and make plans for intimacy and commit to them. It may not necessarily mean you will get intimate every time, but it will help to have the time set for what is important for both of you and mentally preparing for what may happen next. Leaving room for transitioning will also help set the mood and get ADHD partners ready for their next task rather than remaining hooked on the previous task they were doing. It will be helpful to expand the definition of sex, and although you want to get intimate today, it does not necessarily mean you will do everything you usually do.

Ultimately ADHD needs to be managed if it is affecting your sex life and your life in general. ADHD cannot be looked at as being the whole story and the big problem. Both partners have their parts to play. ADHD does not create new issues; it just exacerbates universal struggles that even non-ADHD couples have to go through. You may define sex in whatever way works for you, but if it is a priority for the both of you, make time for it. Although you may struggle with getting things started, you will generally feel happy afterward.

Chapter 14:
ADHD and Money Management

M oney management can be an issue for people with ADHD. ADHDers tend to procrastinate, be disorganized, and impulsive when it comes to their finances. Sorting out paperwork such as bills and rent notifications can be a burden for people with ADHD. So much so they keep on putting it off until there is no way to avoid it anymore. Financial struggle can have negative implications on people and relationships. This is the number one cause of conflict amongst couples, whether one of the partners has ADHD or not. You must have been accused of impulse spending because of that last-minute decision to buy something that caught your eye in a supermarket window or something more expensive that you thought was worth the splurge. An impulse buy can be as small as a pack of gum or as big as a laptop. Holding impulse spending in check as an adult with ADHD can be difficult, but your bank account and budget will thank you for taking the time to manage your finances and limit impulse buys.

If you have ADHD, you often lose money and time because you are disorganized; remember, time is money. If you live in a country where you are responsible for filing your tax returns, you might struggle to submit these on time. You may misplace receipts or even lose them because you do not have a practical filing system in place. If you find yourself turning to close friends and family to borrow money to cover your debts, you have a money management problem. If you find yourself buying things unnecessarily without considering your set budget and the necessity of these things, it is because of your impulsivity. If you struggle with money management and also happen to have your own business, you might be at risk of filing for bankruptcy. You may pay interest often because you do not make it on time to settle your dues. If you struggle to manage your finances in real-time, it is likely you haven't started planning for your retirement yet. If you are a mother with ADHD, you may struggle with keeping a family budget. It has been proven that stress and sadness can cause overspending. If you are familiar with the above situations, it is time you start to get ahold of your finances and find better ways to manage them.

Tips to improve your money management skills:

- Start by organizing any incoming mail. Sort your bills separately from other correspondence and put your bills where you can see them. This way, you don't lose or forget about them.

- Create a filing system if you still receive bills in the traditional way. Create separate folders and categorize them: home insurance, health insurance, motor insurance, credit card, and so on. Make sure you file every bill immediately as you receive it once it is settled. If you have not paid it out yet, leave it at the same spot where you can see it is still pending.

- Create a workstation where you keep all your files, calculator, checkbook, and so on. This can help you stop looking for things when you need them, and you know where everything you need to keep your finances organized is.

- Create reminders when your bills are due. Set reminders a couple of days before the deadline to make sure you are always settling on time.

- Create rules for keeping paperwork. Make sure you keep receipts for the stipulated time as instructed by law in your country or for as long as you need them. Avoid keeping unnecessary paperwork as this will add to your clutter.

- Try to minimize the use of credit cards. Paying with credit cards can give you an unrealistic notion of how much you are spending. Wherever possible, try withdrawing cash as per your budget and try sticking to that. Having cash at hand can help you manage your spending because you can see how much you have left to spend.

- Keep a record of your earning and spending. Create a table on your laptop or a piece of paper, and list down all your expenses; ideally, you do this monthly.

- Create a budget taking into consideration your income. Dedicate some of your money for leisure activities and impulse buying but be realistic. Allow time to review your spending at the end of the month. You can write down what you spend at the end of the month and compare it with what you have planned to. This means you can eliminate unnecessary purchases and do better the following month.

- Identify your main categories that require budgeting, for example, fuel, parking, groceries, bills, and so on.

- Try to plan by making budgets for months or years to come based on your income. This way you can be realistic about the money you have to spend, especially if you are considering spending more on occasions like holidays or getting new items like buying a new car.

- Try creating direct debits with your bank. You can use this to get a small portion of your salary at the end of the month into a savings account. You can do the same for separate accounts dedicated to paying bills. For example, if you pay your motor insurance once a year but can add up to $600.00 yearly, try dividing that amount by 12, the number of months, and reserve a small portion every month. This way, when your bill arrives, you do not have to reserve the entire amount just to pay this bill from one month's salary. You can end up struggling to make ends meet that month because you did not plan ahead of time. You can do the same for home insurance, condominium expenses, life insurances, and so on. Do not be afraid to use technology to help you budget.

- To reduce impulse buys, try leaving your credit cards at home and only take the set budget in cash with you. Credit cards instigate impulse buying and make it harder to save money. When buying things online, try putting them on your debit card instead. If you made a large purchase on your credit card, get into the habit of writing a cheque to your bank immediately, so you know you have that purchase covered and already paid off.

- Try putting a sticky note on your credit card with your main goal or what you are saving for written on it. So that every time you grab the card to make an impulse buy, you can have a constant reminder.

- If you feel like you are tempted mostly when you get ads online, use certain mobile applications, or go to specific stores, try avoiding your temptations. Remove these apps from your phone and set targets for impulse buys. If you are at a store, try to set a budget; for example, if something is less than $5.00, you can buy it, but if it is more than $100.00, take note of it and go back to the store after a 24-hour time period. If you still think you need that thing, try taking into consideration your set budget for the month, where and how you can use it, and whether you really need it. Try thinking about how often you plan to use it and if you have something already that can perform the same function. You may want to talk to a trusted friend or family member to help you decide whether you need this item. If you did not plan for this in this month's budget, then make room for it in next month's if you still feel you need it.

- When shopping, make a list and stick to it.

- Never go to the supermarket hungry, you will want to buy everything.

- You may want to take a calculator with you to the supermarket to total everything you have in your cart before getting to the cashier. You may use the calculator on your phone.

- Do not be intimidated to negotiate your car insurance or mortgage. Shop around for competitive prices.

- As a woman with ADHD who is often struggling with money management, if you feel your partner can do a better job of this, do not be afraid to hand this duty to him or her. You are not failing yourself and your family by doing so. On the contrary, you are safeguarding your family's finances.

- If you struggle to plan your finances yourself, you may want to consider hiring a professional financial planner or coach to help you with this. Allow money for their professional fee in your budget.

- If you are subscribed to online email lists, unsubscribe. Those emails you get in your inbox certainly do not help your impulse buying. They will have you surf the website to buy what you probably do not need or can go without.

- If you tend to get into expensive hobbies like video gaming, find new inexpensive or less expensive hobbies. Try exploring museums with free entrances, join clubs, explore public parks, get into an exercise routine, and attend public libraries regularly. If you love reading, but you can never stop buying books all the time and are running out of space. Try borrowing books from a library if you probably read a book once and never return to it again. This can save you money and help declutter your space. Try buying books you want to keep a hard copy of or the ones you are likely to want to read more than once.

- If you and your partner wish to control your spending, try keeping separate bank accounts. If your partner is highly organized, it may cause a conflict if you forget to record cheques or fall for an impulse buy.

- If you struggle to create or come up with a detailed budget, try a simple one. That is better than nothing. Try rounding up numbers and budget in the simplest way possible. If you feel like you can manage your budget if you write things down, then draft a table and simply budget.

- Identify the areas where you struggle the most, be it falling for impulse buys, having bouncing cheques, or missing paying bills.

- Identify your goals. Whether you want to save for a car or pay off your credit card debt, it is important to identify your goals; otherwise, you cannot work towards achieving them. Once you have a clear picture of what you want to achieve, you can then figure out how to reach them.

- Try to create a safety net, and when budgeting, try spending less than what you earn. This way, if an emergency comes up that month, you can afford it. Try transferring a certain amount of money into a savings account straight away. If you can afford and still have money to spare, create an emergency account. If you get a fine or your car breaks down, you do not have to eat out of your savings account. There can be times when this emergency account is not used, and that can be further transferred into your savings account.

- Budget your spending based on your income. If you just started your career, allow yourself time to take off and accept the fact that you might not be making enough money to live a champagne lifestyle just yet. Be realistic about your goals.

It also makes it easier to see how you spend your money. Carry a little notebook with you, or find a mobile app that suits your needs, and keep track of all your transactions, big and small. Include everything you purchase or pay for online as well. You can create categories as well. This could include groceries, restaurant meals, drinks, coffee shops, books, movies, fuel, bus fare, and clothing. Watching your expenses can be difficult or irritating at first, but stick with it, even if only for a week or two. If you are married or in a relationship, your spouse or companion can keep track of his or her spending so that you can share notes. If you are single, you may want to have a reliable friend or family member check in with you to ensure you are on track. And if you do not maintain an exact log of every other bill, the details you gather will help you change your financial habits. In the monitoring, provide both constant and variable expenditures. Fixed expenses can be utility bills, loans, and transportation expenses. Variable expenses can be food, fuel expenses, entertainment, and clothing. Add up all the fixed and variable costs. If they exceed your revenue, you need to take a closer look to see where you can save or cut back. Your disposable income is the sum of money left over after all the costs have been met. What you do with your extra cash can be determined by your circumstances and lifestyle desires. You can use it to go out to eat, do home renovations, take vacations, or plan your retirement. You may find it useful to jot down notes or make a collage of a few items you would like to save for. Sort the data or pictures into two categories: essential and non-essential. What are the next three or five things on your must-have list? What is on your list of non-essentials? What stands in the way between where you are now and where you want to be? Once you have this sorted, you can easily identify the problems you have that interfere with getting you what you need or want. Short-term goals can be saving a little every week by eating out less often or settling bills on time to avoid penalties. Mid-term goals can be saving over a longer period for a slightly bigger expense like going on vacation. Long-term goals can be saving for much bigger expenses like retirement or college tuition.

How to Save Money

Saving is one of the most beneficial things you will do for yourself, your families, and your prosperity. Maybe you will need it for a crisis, or maybe it will go toward a down payment on a new home, but knowing you have some extra cash can provide real comfort. Start small if you do not have any savings, and be cautious with yourself until you learn this new habit. If you have a big target, you might choose to open a separate bank account only for savings or one specific goal and have automatic payments taken out of your salary. You can also opt not to get a savings bank card to force yourself to think twice about borrowing money from this account. Motivate yourself by making cutting costs enjoyable and visually appealing. For example, you could make a map with a savings "temperature gauge" and mark it while you save, or you could use your computer to generate a bar graph and monitor your savings every day or weekly. This can work better for larger saving goals. You could also put cash in a special container or an envelope with a snapshot of something you are saving for taped to the back, just to keep it safe before you can get it to the bank. This way, any time you put money in the envelope, you can be aware of your goals. You can do this if you plan to take a trip to whatever destination you please. Since most services and debt payments are made monthly, you can have a monthly schedule. This is usually spending your money before you get it; this way, you know where your salary goes before you are paid and are less likely to spend it on useless things. You can forecast what you need to pay for by looking at your previous expenses or account history. Several applications can assist you in gathering this information. Online credit card applications can also allow you to save electronic copies of receipts and previous purchases. You should sum up the expenses from the previous 12 months and split it by 12 to get the budget you will need to function for every month from now on. You may set weekly or monthly reminders to go over your planned budget. Choose a day during the week to evaluate your shopping schedule and budget daily. I repeat, if you cannot stick to this routine, set reminders or have close friends or loved ones reminding you to do so. If you and your partner are managing your finances separately, try doing this evaluation alongside them to help you stick to the schedule. Determine which bills or expenditures you anticipate having in the coming week. Then, look at the whole month and see which bills must be charged in the coming weeks. Pay all bills that are due in the week.

Have a financial calendar, ideally incorporated in your daily calendar, something you look at every day. Having a visual alert of your bills is beneficial. An electronic or paper calendar that shows all incoming money, as well as the dates of scheduled payments such as rent or lease, bills, taxes, credit cards, groceries, and fuel, can help you stay on track. Some find it useful to organize money management ideas into a timetable that displays financial activities and how long it will take to complete each one. You must build your timeline based on your objectives and habits. This can be incorporated with your calendar or within your app if you use one to manage your finances. You can start by downloading some applications and taking note of the one that works best for you. You may find some to be more user-friendly than others.

Your money management schedule

Create a timeline that you can stick to instead of dealing with a lot of receipts and bills at the very last minute. Collect receipts daily from your wallet and car, log them into your app or spreadsheet and file them, then open physical bills from the mail and set a deadline for each one. Ideally, you do not leave it till the very last day. Put them in order of their due date and keep them where you can see them. Try settling bills weekly and filing them straight away. Mark the ones you settled as PAID. If you do not need the previous bill as a hard copy, discard it to avoid clutter and unnecessary paper. Review your spending at the end of every week. If there is an issue with your spending, you can identify it straight away instead of only becoming aware of it at the end of the month when it is often too late. Make sure you have a look at your bank accounts monthly. Like this, if you see a transaction you did not make, you can make inquiries right away instead of having to look back at three months to try and trace that transaction. You can do this by using your bank's mobile app if they have one. Try balancing your amounts to zero every month to avoid paying charges or being penalized. File your ATM receipts. Once a year, collect your documents for tax filling. This should be easy if you kept your filling organized during the year like you need to. You may want to use software to help you manage your tax returns if you keep them yourself, otherwise outsource it to your accountant. Once your tax payments have been made, keep receipts and proof of payments where you can find them. Make sure you keep records for the period stipulated by law. Once the year is complete and you paid your dues try evaluating the year and how you performed as opposed to what you planned. Identify whether you have reached your goals. Jot down goals you want to be saving toward in the next year, like buying a new car, buying your first home, or saving for that dream vacation. Make sure you identify any ongoing financial commitments you have, like mortgage and car debt, and make a list of the remaining balance until these are paid off. Keep the target date of when these are paid off as a motivator to help you keep your finances organized.

Divide your priorities into steps that you can take on a regular, weekly, monthly, or annual basis. It is useless leaving things at the very last minute because you know very well you may not be able to concentrate on sorting out your spending for the entire month all at one go. Remember that good money management entails paying attention to all the objectives. They are an important part of the financial reporting routine. You will discover that you can master it once you have devised a financial strategy. Consider how good it would feel to be organized: you would not have to worry about your bank account running out of money, being turned down for a loan, or having your electricity cut off because you failed to pay the bill.

Budgeting for special occasions

When budgeting, take into consideration special occasions like birthdays and holiday seasons. You may procrastinate to buy your loved ones a gift and end up buying them something out of your budget and shipping it in a rush, which ends up breaking the bank for you. Instead of buying Christmas decorations every year, try to organize your space and have decorations you can reuse each year; remember to keep them well. The holiday season is not meant for impressing those around you with gifts you did not intend to get because you cannot afford them. This time of the year is for spending precious time with your family and friends. Before buying a gift, spend time reflecting on what that person might like as a gift, what they enjoy the most, and what they mean to you. Try to place yourself in someone else's shoes and try to imagine how they would feel when receiving this gift. If a gift is too expensive because you wanted to make up for forgetting to get them one in the first place, it may make them uncomfortable or put their gift to shame because they bought you something meaningful rather than expensive. If you know your gift cannot get there in time for the occasion, try printing a photo of what you bought them and explain the situation. They know they have a gift waiting for them, and this can also build a connection.

When saving up for your holiday budget, do not just focus on gifts; take dinners and parties into consideration. Consider a budget for cards and new outfits you need to purchase to go to parties and work events. If you want to host a party and need food and new decorations, try to incorporate that into your budget too. If you opt for DIY gifting, try to consider budgeting for supplies. If a project is out of your capabilities or you do not have the time for it, do not commit. This can only add stress, anxiety, and it can ruin your budget if you did not think it through. If you do your holiday shopping online, try leaving things in your online shopping cart for 24 hours at least. If it is a large purchase, try to check in with yourself and identify ways you are going to use to pay for this item. If you want to get something for yourself, try considering if you need it, have space for it, how you will pay for it, and how often you intend to use it. If you still feel like you need to get this gift after a lot of consideration, try consulting with a family member or close friend to help you realize whether this purchase is worthwhile. The idea is to slow down before purchasing because if you make rushed decisions, you are very likely to regret them soon afterward. Instead of trying to buy everyone gifts, prepare Christmas dinners and parties from your November salary, try reserving a small amount from prior months. By the time the holiday season is upon us, you can have your mind at rest that the expenses associated with are already covered.

Having ADHD does not have to result in financial ruin. Start with a plan and work your way forward step by step. Don't be afraid to call for assistance; you don't have to do it all on your own. Also, don't be ashamed. Many adults who do not have ADHD struggle with financial control. You can do it, so step up to the plate and begin.

Chapter 15:
ADHD and Organization

G etting and keeping organized is a real struggle for people with ADHD. Many adults can struggle with clutter in both the home and the workplace, leaving them feeling exhausted or trapped. Getting coordinated will benefit you in various ways, including increasing efficiency, reducing fear, giving up time wasted searching for stuff, and serving as a good role model for your children

Getting tasks underway is one of the most difficult aspects of making a transition. Reward systems or promotions will assist you in being more prepared, as previously stated. Until you begin an organizational project, decide on a prize for yourself after you've completed it. When you've finished the job, make sure to reward yourself. Having a friend assist you will make the job simpler and quicker, especially if you need to declutter. Friends will assist you with getting rid of items because they do not have the same emotional connection to them as you do. You may also find social help in online chat communities. Some have features where you make clear promises to arrange a room, then leave your computer to organize for a while before returning to support each other. You may benefit from using a timer or music. The timer can be programmed to go off in 15-minute intervals, with 15-minute breaks in between. Breaking down a difficult task into simpler steps and tackling these steps one at a time is the only way to master it.

Try the following steps to organize a physical space:

1. Choose the spaces to be organized. Make a list of the areas you want to declutter.

2. Arrange them in descending order of difficulty. You may write these down on post-its and stick them to your refrigerator or on the notice board in your study. Estimate how long each task can take you to complete. Once you establish how long it can take you, try dividing that time into smaller intervals with short breaks in between. Do not pretend to clear a whole room in 3 hours without having a break. You can be headed for failure if you do. Dividing the task into realistic intervals can get you a higher rate of success, and as you might have figured by now, starting is a big hurdle for people with ADHD. Once you start off performing the task, you feel a sense of accomplishment which convinces you to persevere and complete it as planned.

3. Begin with the simplest space. Starting easy can maximize your chances of completing the task and being successful. Because people with ADHD feed off adrenaline rush and stimulation, succeeding at one task can make you more likely to complete the following ones. Divide the room into parts and focus on one at a time, arranging, discarding, or reorganizing each item in that section until it is completed. Dividing the space you want to organize into quarters can be very helpful. You can plan to declutter a quarter of the room in 30 minutes, for example. This can give you a more realistic notion of time and its management. People with ADHD can struggle with this attribute because they have a false sense of time. When organizing your room, try to keep things according to their function. Keep things where you

know you use them and can find them later. If you need cleaning supplies or other things to organize your space, make sure to prepare it before starting on the task. If you need garbage bags or vacuum cleaners, make sure you have them available; otherwise, it can be very easy to get distracted. When clearing your space, decide whether you can get rid of some things, box them, store them away, or keep them handy.

4. Choose an incentive or inspiration to promote the completion of this task. Once you complete the task, make sure you reward yourself.

5. When the smallest room is arranged, work your way up to the most complex, repeating steps if necessary.

Another challenge can be staying organized and maintaining the hard work you have just done. If you work with paper, recycle or trash unnecessary ones. If you can, try working electronically and limit the paper piles. Try using a scanner or an application on your phone to save soft copies of important documents. Create a filing system. Make sure you file every day if possible or as frequently as required to avoid cluttering your space again.

You can create storage space if your area is limited. If you work from your room, try storing work material under your bed or use over-the-door organizers to store smaller things like stationery and pantry items. These would usually hang on the side of a cabinet or a door and helps to create storage space. They are usually made either of fabric or plastic and can be bought from your local store for cheap. Besides creating storage space, they also organize your space and help you put things in one spot. Store things where you are likely to spot them easily when needed. This can save you time and frustration.

Try these tips for staying organized and limit the clutter:

- If whilst you clean, you end up discovering long-lost items and do not know where they go, collect them in a box and after you are done cleaning, try finding them adequate space.

- Work at the moment by putting things away immediately when you realize they are out of order. If you walk by an open drawer, close it. If your wastebin is full, empty it. If you see clothes lying around on the floor, pick them up and put them in the laundry basket straight away. If you notice some papers lying around, file them.

- Take ten minutes from your day to clean up around the house. This small step every day can alleviate the burden of having to devote bigger chunks of your day just to clean up your space.

- The most difficult part is getting started, but once you start and see that you are making gains, you are more inclined to stick with it. Try to adopt a mindset that allows you to believe you will only stick to this task for a stipulated amount of time. Once you start, you are more likely to continue.

- Try eliminating an item before you get a new one. After contemplating whether you can get that item, try eliminating something else that you are not using that much or at all. You may donate items you no longer use or resell them. You may want to keep a box on the side for things you no longer need, and once you have enough items, you can make one trip to the charity shop and donate.

After reading these tips, some readers would be able to begin planning. Others can require the help of a mentor, experienced organizer, or therapist to get started. If you need assistance, do not despair or give up. It took a lifetime to get to the state of disarray in which you have been living; it could take years to repair it. The important thing is to get started.

Chapter 16:
ADHD and Time Management

You are not alone if you struggle to manage your time or follow through with your plans. Many individuals with ADHD discover that a combination of inadequate leadership abilities, poor time control, and difficulties with working memory results in wasted time and unfinished tasks and schedules at work and at home. Adults with ADHD have a different perspective on time. The failure to predict potential incentives and repercussions, as well as the impressive propensity to procrastinate and disregard the static surroundings, all add to the difficulties with schedules, punctuality, and preparation. Individuals with ADHD have the most misery and difficulty getting things done while struggling with time management. The advantage of completing tomorrow's tasks or establishing good work routines now could be the avoidance of complications and indisposition later. Understanding and managing ADHD can change if you consider it to be a matter of time management.

How many times have you said these words to yourself; "I am late", "I am on the way", or "I will be there soon?" It hurts to be late for work, your doctor's appointment, your dinner, meeting a friend, taking the kids to school, and, most of all, picking the kids up from school. How do you break the cycle? What steps would you take to boost your time management? Planning and marking time can be two skills people with ADHD lack. Overcoming this hurdle can mean you need to plan your day every day. Try adopting methods that work to your liking. Use external factors to get a realistic idea of time. Try not to over-schedule.

People with ADHD tend to be people-pleasers and often avoid refusing requests from people or saying no. This can overburden their schedule with no time left for them to relax. Over-planning can set someone up for failure and frustration.

There are various ways to avoid this, so try the following:

- Get hold of a planner that works for you. Consider technology, compatibility, aesthetics, and ease of usage.

- Once you have a planner, block your schedule with things you know you have to do, like attend work, medical appointments, and family dinners. Scheduling activities allows you to see if your day is filled up, which can help you from overcommitting. Rather than making a list of things to do, block out time for each task. If conditions change or something isn't done, it's no huge deal to shift it to another time slot on the calendar. You can see the big picture: the amount of time you have in the day and the things that are starting to take up the time.

- Keep a list of things you want to do and things you must do. People with ADHD can often choose to do whatever pleases them whilst other important things remain unattended to.

- Chose high-priority things to put on your to-do list and jot them down on your planner. Do not overload your day, and be realistic on how much a task can take you to complete.

- If something comes up during the day that must be done, try swapping it for another task. Do not just add things to your day without removing others. 24 hours is not endless, and you need time for yourself.

- If you find yourself surfing the internet more often than you should, try switching off auto-play mode and switch of electronic devices or TVs to help you go to sleep earlier.

- Try to schedule regular check-ins with someone you trust so they can help you stay up-to-date on your time management skills.

- Make your lifestyle a priority. Plan for grocery shopping, meal prep, and exercise during your day.

- Establish a bedtime and a wake-up time to help motivate you to go to bed and get up in the morning.

Leaving the house on time can often be a challenge for people with ADHD. Think of the time you need to make it on time and allow time to get yourself ready and get there. Leave a time window for emergencies or unforeseeable situations like traffic. Establish a station close to your door at home and hold all important things there, your phone, wallet, glasses, and keys. Get ready the night before, prepare clothes, bags, or any items you might need. If you have a false sense of time, which most people with ADHD do, try setting timers for everything you do in the morning to limit the time you spend for every activity like having coffee or taking a shower. Alternatively, you may want to set your time some minutes ahead to ensure you are not late. Allow time for a shower and getting ready, and when your timer goes off, move on; otherwise, you will be late. This can take some getting used to but once done every day, it gets easier. If you think you can stop by a drive-through coffee shop on your way to work, you probably will be late for work again. So, avoid saying you have one last thing to do because that thing can put you behind schedule, a schedule you worked so hard on planning. Take into consideration the time it took you to complete the same task the last time you did it. If you planned for 30 minutes last time but ended up using twice that amount of time, do not repeat the same mistake this time.

Take into consideration time-eaters, those little things that waste your time, but you often do not consider. These can be walking to work from the tube station, getting out of the parking lot, small talk with passers-by, and waiting at elevators. Some people with ADHD end up being late most of the time because they want to avoid getting there early. That can put them in an awkward position and uncomfortable situations. Try leaving things in your car that can help you fill the time if you arrive early, like playing on your phone or reading a magazine. You can also use the extra time to meditate- this can help you recharge your brain and make you more productive during the day. If you always put off cleaning your wallet or your purse, use this time to do so.

Many with ADHD are strongly affected by their surroundings; those without find it easier to ignore environmental stimuli. Neurotypicals may use their executive functions to make decisions based on their interests. The further away from a possible incentive or penalty, the less inspired people with ADHD are by it. On Monday, a Friday deadline means little. A set alarm clock for 6 am does not mean people with ADHD get in bed at 10 pm. They know what they have to do but struggle to do it. If performing a task takes longer, people with ADHD may put it off because the reward is farfetched. Similarly, if the deadline is not in the coming hours, they are very likely to keep putting off working on that project because they are not encouraged by deadlines or penalties. Many people with ADHD are unaware of potential events and implications as they do not appear on their internal radars until much later, and if a mission is on their agenda, they cannot complete it. This makes them too reliant on the burden of the approaching deadline and, as a result, free to procrastinate. And if they are aware that they should begin sooner, they do not feel the burden fast enough. Meanwhile, the present's temptations build an unequal battle, and the future has a difficult time winning. The more clearly you can recall past emotions and outcomes, the more motivated you can be to make changes in the future.

You can find yourself arriving on time, if not early, and feel much more comfortable and content the next time you use these tips. Time management may seem to be a hazy, alien phenomenon, but it boils down to a tug of war between maximizing the current benefits and maximizing the prospects. Time is money; being late costs you money, so think of the things you can do with that lost money, and you can soon be on the way to better managing your time.

Chapter 17:
The Good Side of ADHD in women

Many people just see the many issues associated with ADHD and believe the media and society's misinformation and negativity towards it, seeing it solely as a flaw, and are unaware of ADHD's strengths. Do not confuse your ADHD qualities with symptoms! They are distinct characteristics and abilities that make you more imaginative, spontaneous, compassionate, and enthusiastic than anybody else you meet. Be proud of your ADHD and all the creative thinking, humor, drive, and excitement it offers. Not all women with ADHD have the same personality characteristics, but certain personal qualities can turn ADHD into an asset rather than a disadvantage. Research into the benefits of ADHD is often dependent on stories about individuals with ADHD rather than studies. Anyone who has this condition says that it has improved their lives if the characteristics are turned into strengths and used in the right environment. There is a widespread belief that people with ADHD are too busy to get things done. Nothing may be farther from the facts.

Here are some of the characteristics for ADHD which can be considered an advantage rather than an impairment:

Hyperfocus- ADHD's signature hyper-focus is a significant gain, provided you can successfully redirect all your attention and commitment into meaningful practice. Many scientists, researchers, and artists with ADHD have had very fruitful careers, thanks mainly to their willingness to concentrate on what they are doing over long periods. If you enjoy doing something so much you focus on it excessively, this can be an advantage because it means you will get things done. This causes them to get so focused on a mission that they do not know what is going on around them. The advantage of this is that if a person with ADHD is assigned a task, they will concentrate on it till it is completed without losing focus, spending hours of undivided attention and concentration on an assignment. You may get into a trance and become fully lost in what you are doing as the outer world fades away.

Energetic- Some people with ADHD appear to have an infinite supply of energy that they can turn into progress on the playing field, in education, or at work. Some jobs or activities require copious amounts of energy, and where neurotypical brains can often feel drained after a 12-hour shift, someone with ADHD may still be going strong at the end of their shift. The high-tech world's rapid transition, for example, may be exhausting and upsetting for some people, but it's also exciting and energizing for the ADHDer because it is a fantastic source of dopamine. Your brain works at a breakneck pace to absorb information. You can do something on a machine in 30 minutes that might take others hours. The energy ADHDers have can help motivate those around them and help keep everyone focused and enthusiastic about the set goal.

Resilient- People with ADHD succeed at overcoming obstacles, implementing new tactics, and getting on further than ever before. ADHDers have failed multiple times before becoming successful, and this failure has turned them into persistent individuals. They are used to things not going to plan, so they learn to adapt and keep trying harder. They tend to be the ones working on solutions when everyone else around them is freaking out. They have developed perseverance and stubbornness to just keep going, even if it feels like swimming against the current.

Enthusiastic- Because of emotional dysregulation and because of the dopamine kick people with ADHD strive to experience, they can get excited about the little things and celebrate small successes often. This characteristic can be very beneficial both for the ADHDer and those around them when in the right environment.

A glowing personality- Individuals with ADHD are brilliant, imaginative, and funny, and they often use self-deprecating humor to show the world that perfection is completely uninteresting. They have overcome obstacles, discovered new ways to treat their symptoms, and gained a sense of modesty and self-respect along the way. All these characteristics add up to a person who is a joy to be around and brightens the days of others with their warmth.

Generous- People with ADHD tend to please those around them and care so much about others. They are always ready to help primarily because they understand what they are used to going through emotional turmoils themselves and would not wish it on others. They tend to be very compassionate and empathetic, hence always available to lend a helping hand. ADHD individuals can offer a helping hand without overwhelming others but ensure they are there if needed and are patient with others.

Fair- People with ADHD who have lived with making adjustments or who have struggled without them understand that "fair" does not necessarily mean "equal." They realize that different people need different aspects to excel, and they are dedicated to assisting everyone they can.

Spontaneity- Anyone with ADHD can be able to turn their impulsivity into immediacy. They may be the life and soul of the group, or they may be more open and eager to explore new ideas and break away from the status quo. This characteristic is what makes things generally boring become interesting.

Humorous- People with ADHD who are well-adjusted have learned to use laughter to deal with stressful situations, relieve tension, reinforce relationships, change minds, and more. Because they have been through a lot of experiences neurotypical brains have not experienced, like storing their wallet in the refrigerator or losing their credit card twice a week, they learn to take every situation as it comes. Laughter helps people with ADHD get through their daily challenges, making life fun for them and those around them. The situations women with ADHD find themselves in cultivates the ability to have a humorous character.

Creative and inventive- While further research on ADHD and creativity is needed, it appears that there is a connection between ADHD and increased creativity. Living with ADHD provides a person with a new outlook on life and allows them to view activities and circumstances with a more reflective approach. Consequently, some ADHD people can be creative thinkers. Other terms that may be used to characterize them include original, imaginative, and innovative. This characteristic can be either learned or otherwise developed because people with ADHD must always find their way through a world that is not always very ADHD-friendly. They tend to think outside the box and find solutions where others cannot. . This comes effortlessly to ADHDers, while others would spend thousands of dollars to master it. In certain careers thinking outside the box can be an asset, and people with ADHD tend to shine in these positions. They have a stream of ideas, and although they might struggle to finish every idea that comes to their mind, they love to create and can often instigate new projects for others to work on and finalize, especially when working as part of a team. Since you take in more detail than the average human and are easily distracted, you are more inclined than neurotypical brains to approach a problem from several different perspectives and thus come up with far more potential solutions to a problem. People with ADHD thrive on variety, transition, and disorder. They can seamlessly construct order from chaos.

Willing to risk- ADHD brain can jump headfirst into challenges and opportunities a neurotypical brain is unwilling to do. Therefore, many ADHD brains opt to open their own business or become self-employed. Neurotypical brains may remain employed because they cannot pluck up the courage to open their own business either because they have not come up with an innovative idea or rather not risk what they perceive as safe. Often, innovative business ideas and risks would work for people with ADHD, take the founder and chairman of IKEA, for example. ADHD allows you to note more details and discover facts and resources that some overlook. It also encourages you to see potential challenges and possibilities that others can miss. Impulsivity indicates that you are more likely to take chances and have a bias towards action;

strike now when the iron is hot rather than being paralyzed by analysis paralysis.

Forgiving- ADHDers are very self-conscious and know they are not perfect. Because of this, they are very understanding of other people's flaws. People with ADHD know that being a good person does not mean you need to be perfect.

Surprising- ADHDers are full of surprises, and both themselves and those around them, do not know what they are going to say or do next. Everyday life can be an adventure if you have ADHD. This can be an asset in relationships as well. You will never live the same day twice, and you can often choose to surprise your loved one with a weekend getaway or a road trip. This can help keep the relationship alive and show that you care for your other half. This can mean you are willing to put in the work to make things last.

Rapid learner- If it is something that piques your curiosity, you are fast to grasp it or the concept of it. ADHD is mostly a boredom disorder; if anything is important to you, you have no problem paying attention to it. Being an information junkie may be beneficial in the right situations.

Work well under pressure- Pressure and deadlines give ADHD brains the dopamine kick they are after. Women with ADHD tend to hyper-focus and get motivated to finish tasks and reach deadlines when under pressure. They can often procrastinate and put things off till the very last minute for this reason. They always assume they have more time than they really do, and when things get real, they can work very well under pressure. Others may panic and fail to meet expectations under pressure.

Singer Justin Timberlake, actor Channing Tatum, actor Jim Carrey, actor Will Smith, and athlete Michael Phelps all have two things in common, they all have ADHD and are very successful personalities who have made it despite what everyone might have told them growing up. An individual with ADHD may need assistance in harnessing these characteristics to their advantage. Teachers, psychologists, therapists, and parents all have a part to play. They must assist a person with ADHD in exploring their artistic side or devoting energies to completing a mission. An ADHD diagnosis does not have to place a person at a disadvantage in life. Instead, ADHD may and has helped many artists, athletes, and business people succeed. Many individuals with ADHD have hit the top of their respective careers. ADHD is a highly manageable disorder, with a variety of approaches available to improve a person's attention and behavior. Medication and rehabilitation are examples of these. People with ADHD who are taught adaptive approaches to assist with time management and organization skills are likely to reach higher levels of focus.

ADHD is not a failed version of a neurotypical brain; they just work differently. It is best to focus on what you have done right than what you have done wrong. Differences in ADHD need to be seen as strengths and not failures. ADHD individuals must keep in mind that they are not alone, and they form part of a community that is constantly striving to make this world more ADHD-friendly and make ADHDers feel accepted and appreciated. The reality, as I've countlessly repeated, is that when people with ADHD discover something they are excited about, they will work harder than anybody else might ever think, sometimes smashing the challenge. Based on what other people have done, I believe it is fair to assume that it should be seen as a strength rather than a weakness.

Chapter 18:
Postmenopausal Women with ADHD

M enopause is a natural phase in a woman's life where her menstrual cycle eventually stops. Menopause can occur at different stages in a woman's life, and not everyone experiences it at the same age. A woman would go into menopause primarily because her ovaries have stopped producing hormones, mainly estrogen and progesterone. Testosterone levels, the follicle-stimulating hormone, also known as FSH, and luteinizing hormone, also known as LH, also fluctuate during menopause. A woman is thought to reach menopause when she fails to have a menstrual cycle for one year. Estrogen levels are said to drop drastically during this period, and those going through this phase may experience irregular menstrual cycles, hot flushes, vaginal dryness, mood swings, and trouble sleeping. These symptoms are experienced by most women regardless of whether they suffer from ADHD or not. But having ADHD surely does not help to get through this natural event. Menopause may at times be induced in cases of surgical removal of the ovaries, pelvic radiation, or hormone therapy. Blood tests can be a way of knowing whether you have entered the perimenopausal stages, whereby you would experience lighter symptoms of menopause. Menopause is also associated with osteoporosis, fractures, changes in cognitive behavior, mood changes, and loss of libido. Measuring levels of hormones in the blood can help determine whether you are currently going through menopause.

Women who have ADHD and start getting into menopause confess experiencing confusion, difficulty multitasking, memory struggles, and general cognitive difficulties. Some might suspect developing Alzheimer's or dementia. Someone who is already on ADHD medication and was controlling their condition may find that whatever used to work just fine for their ADHD may not be sufficient when menopause hits. This is because ADHD combined with lower levels of estrogen can cause an overwhelming feeling. Women who get diagnosed with ADHD at a later stage might experience regret and remorse when looking back at the things they could have achieved if they got the help and treatment they deserved. They would have suffered fewer years of self-abuse and treating themselves as if they were complete failures, lazy, and stupid.

Estrogen affects the release of serotonin. This is the key hormone that stabilizes your mood and helps your brain cells to communicate. This will affect digestion, sleeping, and eating habits. Lack of serotonin can be the cause of depression and anxiety. You can help increase levels of serotonin in the brain naturally; by exposing yourself a little more often to bright light, exercise, meditate, get massages, and consume certain foods. Serotonin is not readily available in food sources but is found in its amino acid form, tryptophan which is converted into serotonin in the brain. Consuming nuts, seeds, spinach, salmon, and eggs can help increase tryptophan levels naturally. Low levels of estrogen during menopause causes even lower levels of dopamine in the brain, exacerbating the symptoms of ADHD. Certain treatment that would usually or mostly work for college students with ADHD may no longer be as effective for menopausal women with ADHD. This is because the decrease in dopamine stems from hormones and not from ADHD. Controlling your ADHD can be crucial in women with perimenopausal symptoms. If your ADHD is not controlled, it will be very difficult to identify the issue and why you are experiencing such symptoms. If your ADHD is controlled, then one can easily rule it out as the root cause of your current symptoms. Increasing ADHD medication will not help in these cases because nothing is being done for low estrogen levels.

One would hope that by the time you reach menopause, you would have also received adequate treatment for your ADHD. At this point, your ADHD is controlled, but minimizing the symptoms of menopause can help control your ADHD as well. It is suggested that loose, layered, and light clothing is worn to help manage hot flushes. Avoiding heavy blankets and keeping the bedroom cool can also help with this. If you experience hot flushes even during the day, try carrying a small portable fan to help with this. Regular exercise can help with increasing energy, promote better sleep, and improve your mood. Physical activity, even for 30 minutes daily, can help promote general well-being and help control your weight. If you are experiencing massive mood changes and going through periodic episodes of depression or anxiety, speak to a therapist and make sure your family members or loved ones are aware of what you are going through. Vitamins can help to supplement your diet during menopause. Calcium, Magnesium, and vitamin D supplements can help reduce the occurrence of osteoporosis or slow its progression. This will also improve sleep and energy levels. Although some of these supplements can be found over the counter, it is best to consult a healthcare professional before adding them to your daily regimen. The same goes for natural sleep remedies, like melatonin. If you are experiencing sleep issues, try consulting a professional to help control your sleeping patterns. Irregularities in melatonin production can cause depression, but in the right amounts, it can help create a healthy sleeping pattern. Yoga and meditation can also help ease stress.

Because during menopause, women tend to experience skin dryness, it is suggested that moisturizers are used daily. Avoiding excessive bathing or swimming can help lessen skin dryness and irritation.

If you feel like completing certain tasks at work has become a challenge, try bartering them with someone else at the office. If you forget to make phone calls daily, try asking a colleague if she can complete them for you, and in exchange, you can do some of her tasks. Try finding the root cause for what is making you forget or avoid making phone calls. You may want to keep a clean working area to avoid clutter and confusion. Prepare for phone calls before making them, so you avoid forgetting what you need to say. If emails work better for you, try encouraging your clients to contact you via email. If you can delegate more work to ease the workload, go ahead and do it. Do not feel like a failure because you are not doing everything on your own; you should not. You need to understand that those around you are part of your support system and are there to share your burden. If what you need to work better is a strategy, use the help of those around you to set one up. If you feel like you already have too much work, learn to say no to new responsibilities or negotiate a better deadline. Writing to-do lists will help you get into the right mind frame for the day. If your day is over and you know you have left so many unfinished tasks, try jotting them down one by one in order of importance and priority. Once you have that done, clear the clutter to start afresh the next day. With a to-do list set, your day is already planned and will help you stay focused longer. Strick things off the list when you are done, and keep with this habit if it works for you. If one task is complicated or you are sure you will not complete it the next day, divide it into smaller tasks and try completing those mini-tasks to keep up with goals and deadlines. If you work in a dynamic office environment where your superiors fire duties and tasks to you as they make their morning coffee in the staff canteen, get into the habit of carrying a small notebook and pen with you wherever you go. You will be able to write down tasks, instructions, and deadlines when this happens. If you feel unsure about the goal objectives, try asking your boss to email you the assignment in detail later so you can have something to look back to while completing the assignment and be sure you do not miss any important details.

Although this tip may not work for everyone, it can help to take it under consideration. You may want to hire a professional organizer who will help you declutter your space and keep you accountable. It is easier to stay on track when you have a professional reminding you all the time. Cognitive behavior therapy can also help in increasing self-control and self-esteem, two factors negatively impacted during menopause.

Menopause cannot be avoided, but by keeping track of any menstrual changes, mood changes, and sleep disturbances, you will soon start to notice these changes and have a record of them. This will give you an indication of where you stand, and with that information at hand, you can discuss your ADHD symptoms and menopausal ones with your psychiatrist, therapist, gynecologist, or physician. ADHD will not disappear with time but knowing how to manage it based on the different stages of life is key to keep it under control.

Chapter 19:
Pregnancy and Children of a Mother with ADHD

P regnant women who also have ADHD may report a drop in their ADHD symptoms. This is because estrogen levels spike during pregnancy. Estrogen targets the brain, helping with dopamine and other neurotransmitters. Keep in mind that ADHD is a spectrum, and some symptoms may be more grievous in some individuals than others. Pregnancy and the estrogen fluctuations it brings with it might help lessen the ADHD symptoms, but that does not make it disappear completely or even cure it. Once pregnancy is over, estrogen levels will plummet again, causing ADHD symptoms to return, in some cases with more intensity—some report experiencing post-natal depression and anxiety. With becoming a parent, one must keep in mind this is a process and a life-changing event in itself, might I add. ADHD will impact you and your child whether you have it diagnosed or not.

Pregnancy and ADHD

Women may have a planned pregnancy, but some may get pregnant unexpectedly. Ideally, women with ADHD who also happen to be on medication for this condition would discuss and contemplate whether to stay on ADHD medication during pregnancy before getting pregnant. At this stage, women planning to get pregnant together with their physician and partner would weigh in the risks and benefits of getting pregnant and seizing ADHD medication versus continuing with treatment just the same. Women with ADHD who decide to alter or seize their ADHD medication may also need to continue doing so during breastfeeding. In most cases, this decision is taken after the woman learns she is pregnant, which would usually be four or more weeks into the pregnancy. At this stage, the fetus would have already been exposed to medication. None of the treatments used in ADHD is proven to be safe in pregnant women, but there is no confirmation of them being unsafe either. There has never been an ethical way of conducting studies for the safety of such medication on pregnant women and the outcome on their babies to date. This leaves both physicians and expectant mothers at a crossroads. A physician would usually decide based on their knowledge, the documented outcomes of similar situations, and their best judgment for their patient. They consider the woman with ADHD, the severity of her condition, and other environmental variables. Seizing ADHD medication for a pregnant woman will affect her directly, her baby, her family, and those around her. Because medication passes through the placenta and to the fetus, this will expose the baby to stimulant medication in the womb. Many researchers are trying to gather information about these effects. To date, stimulant medication is harmful to the fetus based on animal studies carried out. There is a record of women continuing their ADHD treatment while pregnant for observational purposes because actual trials cannot be conducted for ADHD medication during pregnancy. A designated office forming part of the Food and Drug Administration still gathers this data and keeps a register for it. This information gathered is factual and is there to teach more about medication during pregnancy. Although these studies are not accurate for pregnant women who are about to decide whether to continue their ADHD medication during pregnancy, results show a high infant mortality rate and preterm deliveries. These results cause many physicians to advise against continuing their ADHD medication through their pregnancy. Some may choose non-pharmacological treatment for women with mild to moderate ADHD who happen to be pregnant. Exercise, cognitive behavior therapy, diet, and dialectical behavior therapy can be an option. The latter is a type of cognitive behavior therapy that aims to teach people to cope with stress, control their emotions, improve their relationships, and helps them live in the moment rather than worry about past or future events in life they have no control over. Cognitive behavior therapy will help with awareness and change problematic patterns of behaving and reasoning. Whether or not an expectant mother continues her ADHD treatment will be based heavily on her needs for the medication and her inclination to not expose her unborn baby to drugs that we know very little about when taken during pregnancy. If an expectant mother with ADHD decides to stop her medication, those around her should be made aware. Symptoms of inattention, hyperactivity, and impulsivity may return during pregnancy and when off medication. People at work, family members, and friends may be taken off guard by this. They can also offer help and be your support system if you involve them in your decision. Decreasing your responsibilities during this time is beneficial. Women who take medication for their ADHD may find it difficult to transition to a period where they are off their medication and pregnant. Especially during maternity leave, expectant mothers tend to spend their last few days before giving birth at home. Staying at home a lot would not help, especially when you are off medication. Managing a business from home or doing simple house chores can also prove to be challenging without the help of your usual ADHD medication. ADHD treatment tends to build up in one's system, so once you stop the treatment, you would not experience symptoms straight away. This is subjective and depends on the dosage one would have been on before seizing treatment. During the first months of pregnancy, a neurotypical woman would experience a stir of emotions caused by the pregnancy itself, so being a woman with ADHD who is also off her treatment may experience an even bigger emotional turmoil once the effects of the medication start to wear off. They may struggle with emotional overload and may also find it hard to control it. Pregnant women off treatment may feel tired, demotivated, experience suicidal thoughts and depression. When an ADHD brain has nothing to focus on or is not stimulated by anything, it may feel like shutting off, hence making the neurodiverse individual feel tired more often. Impulsivity may also be an issue for expectant mothers who stopped their ADHD treatment and so sticking to healthy eating practices and incorporating physical exercise may be slightly difficult to stick to.

If you are a woman with ADHD who just discovered you are pregnant and happen to be impulsive because of your ADHD, then it is best if you start adopting healthy eating habits to avoid impulse eating. This will help you avoid complications in pregnancy associated with your diet, like gestational diabetes. Setting time aside for food preparation can help with impulse eating as well. Make sure you make frequent grocery trips to ensure a good amount of healthy food is always available during your 9-months. Pre-natal vitamin intake is crucial during the first trimester, and remembering to take your vitamins can be very challenging if you have ADHD. Try setting up alarms on your phone, have a stash of vitamins in areas you will remember to take them, like in your bag, at work, and at home. Allow yourself to feel tired and permit yourself to rest because you are most definitely going to need it.

Discuss budgeting ways with your partner, so you will not find yourself struggling to get the supplies you need at the very end of your pregnancy. If you are taking time off work and find yourself bored at home, try reading pregnancy books. With ADHD, it may be very easy to lose focus but reading about a stage you are going through at this very moment can help you keep your focus and teach you handy tips along the way. Socializing can also help you get the support you need from your family and friends whilst also enjoying some time out. If you are an introvert, you may not opt for this last tip, which is perfectly fine. At the end of your pregnancy, you may want to start getting all the things you need for yourself and for the baby to come. You may also take setting up a nursery as a project. Taking prenatal classes can also help you during this special time in your life. Try avoiding triggers that would stress you out because emotional reactivity can be a struggle in itself for women with ADHD, let alone if you are also pregnant. Experiencing stress during pregnancy can also negatively impact the baby, so it is best to avoid this altogether. It is very important to be kind to yourself and understand that pregnancy can be a struggle for neurotypical brains and even more so for neurodiverse ones. Yoga or meditation for pregnant women can help alleviate the symptoms of ADHD.

Breastfeeding and ADHD

Research and data on women with ADHD and breastfeeding on medication are lacking. ADHD treatment should only be taken if the potential benefit justifies the potential risk to the baby. Some physicians give a lot of importance to breastfeeding, which may vary from country to country as traditions tend to diversify. Doctors who emphasize breastfeeding and its benefits to the baby may encourage nursing mothers to discontinue any unnecessary medication as traces of these drugs may come up in the mother's milk. A physician may opt for short-acting medication for ADHD rather than a long-acting one. This will help the medication to peak quickly in the blood and last for a lesser amount of time. This can be achieved by switching from sustained-release medication to immediate-release medication. In these cases, the dosing schedule can be modified to fit the mother's and the baby's feeding and sleeping schedule. Immediate release medication can help reduce the exposure of treatment to the baby. With this treatment, drugs can peak for about two hours and will mean that during this time, the drug is highly present in the mother's blood and can be transferred easily to the baby during lactation. With sustained-release medication, the levels of medication in the blood rise at a slower pace and will remain available for longer, usually about 8 hours. Choosing to lactate before taking the medication can work better with immediate-release medication but not sustained ones. Mothers may nurse their child before taking the dose, leaving a lessened possibility of passing the ADHD medication effects on the baby. This can become easier as the baby grows older as they tend to lactate less often, leaving the mother with a bigger window of availability for her to take her drugs. Because a baby's liver is less capable of breaking down medication, drugs secreted into the mother's breast milk can take longer to be cleared in a baby than an adult. This makes the baby more susceptible to adverse drug effects. This will also depend on whether the baby is exclusively breastfeeding or also taking formula milk or solid foods. If this is the case, they would be taking less breastmilk and therefore are less exposed to traces of ADHD medication. If the mother opts to stay on ADHD medication while lactating, she may want to work closely with the pediatrician to monitor any reactions caused by the negative effects of her medication. A parent may notice irritability, abnormal weight gain, agitation, changes in feeding habits, and poor sleeping habits in their child. They must speak to their doctor and consider lowering the dose or stopping treatment altogether if this is the case. When a woman with ADHD decides to stop her treatment when she first becomes aware of her pregnancy, she might also be prepared to not take her medication at all, even after giving birth. Some physicians may ask expecting mothers to try getting off their medication whilst pregnant and allow them to start back on if they need to. If this is the case, then the mother may continue with ADHD medication throughout the pregnancy and follow through the nursing period as well. This will need to be discussed with your doctor to find the best possible solution for your condition and the baby.

Parenting and ADHD

It is very common for children to be diagnosed with ADHD, and the diagnosis of one of the parents follows right after. ADHD can be hereditary. It might be very well established by now that women will often get misdiagnosed at their early ages. The stigma surrounding adulthood ADHD and the lack of understanding certainly doesn't help. Parenting can be overwhelming, and parents with undiagnosed ADHD may find it harder to meet their children's requirements. They may lack organizational skills, struggle to keep with their kid's schedules and find dealing with their behavior very stressful. They forgot to get kids their school supplies on time, picking them up late from school, forget to take them to extra-curricular activities, and fail to provide a harmonious environment at home.

It would be ideal for a mother with ADHD to get diagnosed because it will benefit them and their kids, drastically improving the quality of life for them and their families. Kids with ADHD require a caregiver who can handle the scheduling of appointments, fill prescriptions for controlled drugs, take care of health insurance or manage whatever health system is applied in their home country, monitor side effects, and make sure medication is being taken as it should. If the caregiver has ADHD and is uncontrolled or undiagnosed, doing all this besides taking care of the home and the rest of the family can be challenging and nearly impossible. A child's treatment requires compliance and consistency to achieve results. It is relatively obvious that this cannot be achieved by the child alone. Mothers with ADHD may know what needs to be done but have a hard time carrying tasks out. Parents with ADHD can benefit from getting a diagnosis because it will alleviate stress and reduce the level of guilt they impose on themselves and allow them to focus more on the genetic disorder they have, the same as their child does. They will understand where everything is coming from and will get the treatment they need. A mother with ADHD who is also receiving the right treatment will notice an incredible improvement in her parenting skills and a reduced load on the entire family. If you can become organized and stay organized, you will be able to give more attention to your kids. Feeling more relaxed and comfortable with their children is what every mother hopes to attain. Cognitive behavior therapy can be a great accompaniment for ADHD medication for both the kid and the mother. If both you and your child have ADHD, you probably struggle to pick up their toys or minimize their clutter. Apply the same techniques you use for yourself and set a timer for them to clear the clutter, give them something to look forward to, and set a deadline for them. Write routines for kids so they know what to follow. Set the tone every morning and try to stay positive; it is likely to carry on during the day. If they struggle to complete their tasks try helping them with their homework, it can help them get over that hurdle while you also spend quality time with them. Organize your kids' medical records in binders, color-coded if you wish, and make one for yourself too. You might have bills that are due as well, but if you need their medical records, which you will very often, you know where to find them. Try to avoid picking fights unnecessarily; if their socks do not match every morning, cut them some slack and think back to what you did as a child, it can help you understand them.

Chapter 20:
Best Jobs for Women with ADHD

An ADHD brain can have unique attributes considered to be an asset in certain jobs. There is no one-size-fits-all career for either neurotypical or neurodiverse brains, but there are jobs that would fit better for women with ADHD. Having said this, there are no jobs ADHDers cannot perform, but there are some environments and careers that will help people with ADHD to thrive rather than struggle in their job posts. ADHD symptoms can cause difficulties in the workplace for adults, just as they do for children in school. Adults with ADHD will have a very promising career. Others can face several difficulties, such as poor listening skills, distractibility, procrastination, and trouble handling complicated tasks. Seeking advice from an occupational coach, nurse, social worker, or other health care worker with career therapy experience will help you understand and cope with ADHD at work. Each person with ADHD faces a unique set of challenges. As a result, it is essential to remember your specific image when developing plans, accommodations, and modifications for the job.

If you have ADHD and are struggling at your current employment or feel like you do not fit the bill at your current post, have a look at this career list: -

Journalism-This is a creative and dynamic environment to be part of, and the inattention issue will not be a problem here. The fast-paced environment will have you working on different stories all the time, and because you probably function better under pressure, you are likely to find this career role a better fit for you. Journalists also interact with a lot of people and will need to deliver a quick turnaround. Keeping to tight deadlines can, however, be a challenge for some women with ADHD, but that can be overcome.

Copy Editor- This is very similar to journalism because you would be set up to work on multiple stories at once and will need to deliver work within fast and tight deadlines. Working on an array of different stories will help with your inattention as well.

Hairstylist-You are working on different clients who are after different hairstyles, colors, and looks. This environment is very casual and social, and creativity plays an important role in this career. A lot of hairstylists might wish to open their salon, and this is also one of the ADHD traits- wanting to be their boss. This role has many diverse tasks that will keep you focused on the client at hand. This role also has plenty of room for growth because you can strive to make a name for yourself.

Beauticians- Beauty salons have different clients walking in, each asking for different services, which usually require creativity and focus for a short time. They also tend to work long hours and may be required to work outside shop hours during weddings or special occasions. Having a packed schedule leaves less time for boredom and gives plenty of opportunities for social contact. This job post is also ever-changing because new techniques come in regularly.

Doctor- Becoming a doctor requires you to be over-ambitious, and that is exactly what ADHDers are. Doctors need to multitask well under pressure, and this might be overwhelming for the neurotypical brains but not the ADHD ones. In a doctor role, one needs to be creative to handle different emergencies under pressure. ADHD tends to live on emergency mode all the time, so it fits the bill perfectly. Graduating from med school is not easy for anyone, but if young girls with ADHD are passionate about medicine and health, they will hyper-focus on the one thing that interests them.

Nurse- Nurses tend to work very long shifts and need to stay focused because a mistake on their side can cost somebody's life. They are very aware of this and are happy to be assigned responsibilities. If a nurse needs to be in surgery or help prepare medication for patients, they can stay focused on the task and deliver. Because a hospital is bustling with patients and duties to be completed, nurses often are worked up, and if you are a neurotypical brain, you might lack enough energy to complete your 12-hour shift.

The entertainment industry- Jobs in this industry are usually very vibrant and ever-changing. This will require you to put your absolute best in each role, kind of like hyper-focus! Once you are done with this role, you can move on to the next and put the same time and effort into that. Anyone who thrives in creative chaos will find themselves opting to work in a fast-paced and artistic environment. This can be as a TV producer, pianist, choreographer, dancer, or actor. Theatrical stage managers are required to facilitate production, including rehearsals and meetings. No two days are the same, and entertainment industry workers are required to maintain their focus in a dynamic environment. This career also calls for creativity, something women with ADHD do not struggle with!

Teacher- Adults with ADHD tend to find satisfaction in careers that allow them to be dynamic and creative. This might also mean that your patience is put to the test, which is expected when working with kids. Transitioning from one task to the next and understanding the strengths of kids in your class who have ADHD as well may be a plus.

Childcare worker-This is very similar to teaching but will allow people with ADHD to be even more creative and switch tasks constantly because the syllabus at childcare centers is less academic and more creative. Having a lot of energy is also very important when working with kids who themselves are bursting with energy.

Owner of small businesses- Being your own boss can help you thrive as a woman with ADHD. You can oversee your schedule and duties. You can pick a business sector that you are most interested in, so you are sure you will be doing what you find interesting and not be forced to stick to whatever is assigned to you. Your own business will be something you create, so hyper-focusing on this will be a plus for you. Your work setup can vary from day to day, and this will accommodate your boredom and restlessness. Having the opportunity to choose your career will make your life more meaningful. Owning a small business and having people work for you can be advantageous if you want to delegate tasks that you know you struggle to perform.

Freelancer- If you have struggled with completing deadlines at your past employment, freelancing might be the right choice for you. You will be free to take up whatever task you feel like you can handle. Clients will want their product or service delivered on time against set requirements. You will get to use your best skills, and because you have a set deadline and clear instructions on how to carry out that task, you might thrive at this as an ADHDer. Freelance is very broad, and you can also do this job remotely.

Emergency first responders- This encompasses police officers, paramedics, and firefighters. All these require the ability to work well under pressure and emergencies. These jobs do not have one fixed setting and have that adrenaline rush ADHDers seek. When neurotypical individuals start to panic in certain situations, neurodiverse individual's brains will kick in and allow problem-solving to complete the task presented to them.

Chef- People with ADHD tend to have a lot of energy and be creative. Chefs work insanely long shifts in a fast-paced environment. Whether they are pastry chefs or manage an a la carte restaurant, attributes of an ADHD brain will go very well in a culinary job. Even if you might not be seeing orders all the time, there is a lot of preparation to be done before service commences. You will also need to keep a good inventory in your pantry and fridge. If you hold a higher post as a chef like a sous chef, you will be given more responsibility, and as a woman with ADHD, this will go very well with your personality. Again if you are in charge, you may be more flexible about delegating tasks you seem to lack in, leaving you with more opportunity to use your strengths instead.

Hospitality industry worker- Very similar to the job above, working in this industry will have you on a very unpredictable schedule. Bartenders and food and beverage attendants will need to switch from one duty to the next whilst also attending to clients. They would be trained and have learned the processes needed to complete tasks at the job, so they have a process to follow and know exactly how to complete that tasks. Operating a bar, for example, will require you to open the outlet ahead of time, prepare for service, make sure you have adequate cash for the day, and when it is time to serve customers, all you must do is complete their orders. Once opening hours are over, you will need to clear your station, make enough preparation for the next shift, and close the cash. All of this is an entire process which once learned, can be easily followed through by ADHDers. If you work in a hotel that forms part of a network of hotels and forms part of the food and beverage department, you are very likely to be asked by your line manager to compete in local bartending competitions to make a name for the hotel and yourselves. This will fuel your energy, and because you must create a cocktail, for example, or a signature drink from start to finish, you will be highly engaged and see this as a target. This will require you to invent the recipe after multiple trials, create a garnish for it, and ultimately put up a show for your colleagues and judges alike. This will keep you focused for the time you invent, create, and rehearse for this competition. This will be an added goal during your career and enable you to use the ADHD traits.

Computer technicians- The frontal lobe of the brain is stimulated by technology in people with ADHD. Computer technicians or IT staff in a company go from one desk to the next fixing technical issues for their colleagues. Solving other people's issues will give you a sense of satisfaction because you will feel valued for your skills.

Software developers- Whether in a company or by themselves, they will create content or troubleshoot programs, websites, or applications. This will help people with ADHD to hyper-focus. They would be assigned diverse, interesting, and hands-on tasks. This will help people with ADHD to stay on track and meet targets. Women with ADHD who wish to opt for this career path may also have the opportunity to work as freelancers and remotely.

Factory assembly line worker- This might be a boring job post for someone who does not have ADHD. Some ADHD brains will work better when they have an ultra-structured career. The process is laid out to them, and they would also have targets to reach during production. Some ADHDers succeed when they have instructions spelled out to them. In most cases, their shift is never the same, and their schedule will vary from week to week, leaving some sort of flexibility in their daily lives. This career may not be ideal for every woman with ADHD, but some line workers can be given more responsibilities and get promoted.

Retail Workers- Whether it is a bookstore or an administration-type post, you are very likely to be busy with clients or tasks most of the time. You have a set of procedures to follow to open and close the outlet, and whenever you are not seeing to clients, you have plenty of stocking up to do, inventory duties, and cleaning. If you work in an office or assist other managerial staff, you are very likely to be given instructions for things to be completed. You are mostly always going to be busy with filing, emails, bookkeeping, and answering phone calls.

Interior designer- This is a hands-on, creative post and will require your creativity. Some ADHDers combine this attribute with problem-solving and often excel in this post. Their brain would be racing with ideas, and they will transpose beautifully in such a role. Thinking outside of the box can be very appreciated in this job post.

Personal trainer- ADHD brains have so much energy to spare, and if they are passionate about sports, this might be a good swap for whatever boring job they are doing now. This will require them to plan training sessions or one-to-one classes for their client. Personal trainers may be using up most of their energy at work, and that will not leave them jumping off the wall at the end of their day because they feel they have not used up enough of their energy at work. This may mean you are a yoga instructor, pilates instructor, do personal training sessions at your client's houses, or are employed at a gym or fitness center.

Mechanic- This is a very technical career that requires you to know how things work. Because vehicles are constantly changing, you will also need to stay ahead of the game and learn new things as you go. At this point, if you have chosen this path, cars are probably your passion. So, whenever a faulty car comes in, you will very likely be invested in fixing it and sticking to a deadline set either by yourself or by the vehicle owner. This will also get you in contact with a lot of people, and you can socialize while you work on what you love. This post may also allow you to work and own the business simultaneously, allowing flexibility in your schedule.

Photographer- This is a very dynamic occupation whether you work with a company or are self-employed. You may be called to work at weddings, baptisms, holy communions, or family events. This job is ever-changing. Learning new techniques and owning state-of-the-art camera equipment will help you build a good reputation. People with ADHD will very likely enjoy doing this because of the characteristics it entails to succeed; focusing on the task at hand, keeping up with new technology and new skills, and it is also very dynamic.

Adults with ADHD will discover that their original career choice does not play to their strengths, no matter how hard they try, and that a shift is needed. Before making a career change try considering the below aspects before you do, and this can help you better pick an alternative career.

Interest- Take into consideration both your leisure and your professional interests. Try listing these down and consult with a career counselor. They can provide a list of occupations that correspond to your likings and what is required to fit the job. It is best to choose a job that interests you for it to last; otherwise, you are very likely to quit or be unhappy.

Skills- List down your skills and achievements. Try to look back at what subject you enjoyed at school. Your counselor will help identify the jobs that your skills can best fit. Skills can be mental, interpersonal, or physical depending on the job and whether it entails dealing with data, people, or things.

Personality- Knowing your personality strengths will help you change your professional habits, broaden your career opportunities, and chart a more promising route to a successful career future.

Values- People place different values on various objects. People are usually accepted to work better and more focused when the job at hand is in line with their ideals.

Aptitude- The ability to gain proficiency in a particular field is known as aptitude. It can seem that these are inherent, but this is not always the case. Aptitudes can be taught as well. An aptitude is the propensity to learn a skill dependent on innate gifts or experience, while a skill is a present ability. This includes reasoning, numerical skills, verbal skills, mechanical or spatial skills, language learning, and accuracy.

Energy levels- Different jobs require different levels of energy to get through the day. Some may go through the day with constant levels of energy daily, while others have fluctuating levels of energy. If you intend to make a career change, try keeping a log of your energy levels either in your notebook or via a mobile app. Check in your energy levels during the day and go back to it at the end of the week. If changes in energy levels are minor, you are likely to go through the day without feeling depleted, but if you have major fluctuations, you are very likely to have trouble completing tasks.

Habits- There are habits at the job that can be either expected or measured up. These often depend on personal traits like reliability, commitment, and attitude. If you are expected to be super friendly at a sales-career job, and you tend to be an introvert, then it is very likely that this job is not for you.

Past experience- There is no more valuable information than the experience you have lived. Try extracting information from your past job posts and evaluate what went wrong, what you should have done better or differently, and what you would not rather be doing again. Consider what you enjoyed doing at your previous job and what you would like to have at your current one. Consider things you disliked and what you would not want to have at the next job. Evaluate the time you spent at the previous job. Did you leave after a few months, or you managed to stay committed for years?

ADHD brains are very passion-fueled and hands-on creative. They are independent risk-takers and work at a lightning pace. Some ADHD brains feel like they work better when their duties are ultra-structured and required to work at a high intensity. For people with ADHD, having a healthy and steady relationship is very important, as much as finding the best job for their capabilities. One needs to keep in mind that at the end of the day, one tends to spend more time at work rather than home. People with ADHD will need a creative outlet, and if they fail to find it, they might fall into a pit of depression. It is important to identify the things you love to do, what you are good at doing, and what people will pay you to do. Anywhere these three overlap, you will find your ideal job. If you currently find yourself in a job that you like and enjoy doing but feel like you have reached full saturation at this post, you might want to speak to your superior and explore ways to use your abilities differently; maybe they can assign different or new tasks to you. Your goal and your boss's goal are probably the same; maximum productivity, so do not be afraid to speak to your manager about this issue.

It is not always suggested that you disclose your ADHD at work, so when in doubt, do not directly spit it out but rather discuss your strengths and weaknesses. This way, they would know where your capabilities fit best. You might feel like using the term ADHD can be used against you at work, so it is best to talk about your personality traits without using the term directly. It is acceptable to ask for adjustments at work, like working with your headphones on, because noise often distracts you. There will be a limit of accommodations that can be done because you must keep in mind you do work in a team, and if your boss had to accommodate everyone, they would no longer keep to a corporate structure with its rules and regulations. So, your best option is to find the right job. There are many ways of coming across as dedicated at work. For example, instead of saying you procrastinate and struggle with getting things done, you may want to rephrase it by saying you work better under pressure, can follow instructions, and will work best with a deadline. Naming your strengths and weaknesses will also put your boss at ease about you because if they tend to not know much about ADHD, they would just think you are unreliable. If you do not need adjustments, then disclosing is not required. If you feel like disclosing your ADHD can have your manager or superior discriminate against you, don't.

Here are some suggestions to help cope with many symptoms of ADHD:

Distractibility- This can be both internal in the form of daydreaming or external, like noises and movement around you. You may benefit from a private cubicle or by working from home. Using earphones and listening to music can also help. If having your own space can seem unfair to others or it is just not possible, then try using unused space like meeting rooms or conference rooms. Divert your phone calls while you work on projects and do not wish to be distracted or set your voicemail to take messages which you can return to later. If an idea pops in your head, try keeping a notebook so you can jot it down and get back to it when you finish what you are doing. If you are in a meeting and know you will be asked about your opinion or ideas, try writing them down instead of impulsively shouting them out when it is not your turn. When your turn comes, you will be able to give feedback and talk about your suggestion in a timely manner. Try performing one task at a time.

Impulsivity- If you struggle with impulsivity and anger outbursts, try using self-talk to control your emotions. Try working with a coach to manage appropriate replies and manage difficult situations. Do not hesitate to ask for feedback and take it constructively to become more aware of yourself. Try to incorporate meditation and relaxation techniques during the day. A 20-minute meditation session as soon as you wake up before work can help you relax. If you know what regularly triggers your impulsivity try to anticipate these situations so you are mentally and emotionally prepared. If possible, try to avoid these altogether.

Hyperactivity- This symptom can be beneficial if your work requires a lot of movement or stamina, but this can be an issue if you have an office job. Try taking frequent breaks from the task that requires you to sit down, keep photocopying tasks for later so you can get up every hour or so. Try filling your water bottle every so often, so you get the chance to walk around and not sit at your desk all the time, but do not seem like you are wasting your valuable time.

Poor memory- If you struggle to remember deadlines, your co-workers are probably irritated to have you on the team. Try taking loads of notes during meetings to go back to them if you forget what was said. Make use of checklists to complete tasks and make sure you have them wherever is visible to you, your desktop, laptop, phone, and post-it notes; set reminders for these deadlines, using every source possible, alarms on your phone and desktop. Make use of a bullet journal and make sure you carry it around everywhere.

Boredom- Unless your brain is really stimulated, you tend to blackout easily, especially when performing routine tasks like filing and scanning. Use a timer to help you focus on that task during that time. Do not try to complete long and tedious tasks at one go; instead, split them into smaller tasks. If taking breaks to walk around is not something you can do at the job, try picking a job that has minimal routine duties.

Time-management- Divide big projects into smaller ones and make sure you set a deadline for each task. This will help you stay motivated and work within the deadline. Cut yourself some slack, and make sure you reward yourself every now and again. Make use of reminders or buzzers on your watch, phone, or computer. If you struggle to remember meetings, make sure you set reminders 5 minutes before, and you can also mentally prepare for the meeting ahead besides being on time. Try being realistic of the time a project can take and do not take over more tasks than you can handle.

Procrastination- If you keep putting things off, your colleagues will hate you for it. If a big project is too much to handle and you keep avoiding working on it, try splitting it into smaller projects and ask your superior for deadlines for these. Keeping you accountable is what can make you want to work on tasks. If you work in teams, try pairing up with someone who has good time management skills to learn from them and help keep you on track. If this is hard for you to do, try working with an ADHD coach so they can help to keep you accountable.

Carelessness- If your job involves paperwork, loads of it, you can struggle to turn files in as expected or maintain an organized filing system. Make sure you handle a paper only once and if you have an administrative assistant at the office, ask him or her to handle that for you if possible. Leave the papers you are using at the time handy; the rest make sure you file them where they belong. Try color-coding your files and use labels to make filing fun and organized.

Interpersonal skills- If you struggle with this skill, you probably offend co-workers unintentionally because you are too honest, talk a lot, or interrupt often. Make sure you ask for feedback from co-workers so you can avoid doing what bothers them. Be more attentive and try to pick up social cues. You will notice when your behavior is angering your colleagues. If you are already working with a coach, ask to address this issue during your sessions and determine what usually leads to these situations. If you absolutely don't work well with others, try choosing an autonomous job.

ADHDers are innovators, explorers, risk-takers, dreamers, creatives, visionaries, entrepreneurs, strong-willed, generous, persistent, amongst so many other good qualities that cannot be bought or taught. The positives of people with ADHD outway the negatives; that can be managed. People with ADHD tend to be people who also like to work and prefer it when they are busy. Your body will tell you when you need to stop. If you tend to work overtime or stay up late working, your body will hint it when you need to stop and get some rest. People with ADHD do not have inferiority of mind, they are simply more creative, and their approach to things is different than that of the neurotypical ones. Some might feel that because of their ADHD, they might struggle with managing workplace pre-requisites; however, some ADHDers report a high level of job satisfaction not despite their ADHD but because of it. ADHD brains can love what they do, and they can succeed at it. If you are at the right job, your position will leverage your strengths. It is very important to find the job you love to juxtapose your strengths and accommodate your shortcomings. People with ADHD tend to take tremendous pride in what they do and do it with a passion. They tend to be very committed and loyal at work if they are treated well and feel that they belong there. People with ADHD will admit the impact their condition has on day-to-day job performance, but it is not insuperable.

ADHDers at work tend to be very distractable, may struggle with managing their time, may be disorganized, be forgetful at times, and tend to get bored easily. Despite this, most employees with ADHD do not disclose their condition to their superiors and do not ask for accommodations.

Here is a recap of all the points addressed above:

People with ADHD may feel like there is never enough time in their day's work. Using timers, alarms, and to-do lists can help you manage your time better. If you feel like you are forgetful or struggle to remember certain details, write everything down. Always have a pen and a notebook available with you. If something comes to mind and you know you will forget it later, write it down and get back to it when you have time. Make use of a planner or a calendar. Block times during the day and plan your day.

If you are in doubt about what interests you, try volunteering or shadowing before you commit. It is to be expected that you might be required to work harder than the average person in some areas but know you will thrive in other sectors where your colleagues struggle.

Chapter 21:
How to improve focus in women with ADHD

W hether at work or home, staying focused may be difficult for people with ADHD. They struggle with staying focused, multitasking, staying organized, get bored easily, forget things often, fail to meet deadlines, and are unable to tune out distractions. Having ADHD will not mean you do not get things done like neurotypical brains, but you just get things done differently. It is about every individual finding their way of dealing with tasks and setting your own goals, and being realistic about what you can manage to get done. Starting a task can be a challenge for women with ADHD, so here are some tips on how to improve focus: -

Avoid distractions- If you are working on a computer, try clearing as many unnecessary windows as possible to avoid getting distracted. If you are working on a video or writing, try opening your window to a full screen to help block any other background functions. Put your laptop or computer in a do not disturb mode; this way, notifications of new emails or messages will not pop up on your screen, causing you to lose your focus. Your phone can be an enemy if you are trying to get things done. Put your phone on do not disturb mode too, and put it away in a drawer if you tend to be tempted to check your messages, only to find yourself 2 hours later scrolling through social media. If it helps, put it on silent or even switch it off.

Take your medication at the right time- It might be beneficial for a woman with ADHD who is on medication to discuss options with their prescribing doctors on how their stimulant medication, if any, can help them work better. This is something your doctor will help you navigate, and talking to them about it can make you more productive if you outline your schedule to your doctor and explore how your treatment can help you perform better.

Set reminders and timers- If you know you must dedicate so many hours to a particular task or several duties at home, for example, try planning your day and set reminders so you can remember you need to do that task. Once you set a reminder and you are ready to start working on the task, set a timer for it. This will help you stay focused, especially if you need to stick to deadlines, but if it is something that you dread doing, this means that when the timer is over, you no longer must do that thing you dislike anymore, for now. The timer will add a little pressure to get you to do things, and you know for how long you must keep at it.

Reward yourself- To follow up on the above tip, you may reward yourself once you complete a task. Be diligent with yourself, and make sure you stick to completing the task before you reward yourself. If you dread doing the laundry or cleaning the house, try to reward yourself with something you enjoy, maybe watch an episode from your favorite show or meditate if that is something you enjoy doing. Women with ADHD tend to be reward-driven, so if you know something you like or enjoy doing is waiting at the finish line, you are very likely to persevere to complete the task at hand.

Write it down- Writing things down can help you remember more and think in a more organized manner. Try having a notebook with you everywhere you go, so whatever comes to mind, whether it is errands you need to run or things you need to do, you can write it down and go back to it later. You might use your phone for this, but some might find it easier if they write things down. It is suggested you keep a notebook next to your bed because you might have an overflow of ideas as you are going to sleep. This interrupts your sleeping habits and may have you working on things you can leave for the next day, at 3 in the morning. You may dump whatever ideas you get in the middle of the night and see to them the next morning. You may tend to struggle with shutting off your brain at night, and adapting this tip may give you a better chance of getting to sleep and having a restful night. It has been proven that our brains process information better when we write by hand instead of electronically. Not having an app to keep your to-do lists is probably more beneficial because you will not get interrupted and distracted by other social media apps or advertisements. A physical notebook will also be there whether your phone has run out of battery or has crashed.

Create checklists- List down the things you know you need to do. It helps to have one big list of things you know you need to do at some point, but it will help if you do a realistic checklist, one you know you can manage to complete. This means you can take things you need to do from your main list and write them down on a smaller list for the day, like that you would be taking a larger goal and dividing it into smaller and reachable tasks. Try making a list of things for the next day so you will get right into it as soon as you are ready to start your day. Prioritize tasks according to importance and deadline.

Ask for accommodations- It is important to know what helps you complete tasks, and do not be afraid to ask for the accommodations you need. If sitting next to a window gets you distracted, try asking for a different seat in class. If there is a quiet area in the office where you feel you can work better, try asking for that desk. If you feel like you work better with headphones on, ask for permission. This is not only at work or at school but also in a relationship. If you feel like the noise at home is a distraction that impedes you from working, try to ask for some quiet time. Let your family members or partner know you need some time alone to get work done. This way, they will know better than to initiate a conversation with you because it will disrupt you.

Know your limits- Knowing your limits also means knowing your capabilities. You will be better off not comparing yourself to others. As a woman with ADHD, it does not mean you are less valuable or you will do less; it simply means that you can do things differently. Knowing where you stand with your skills means you will use them more than trying to compare yourself to others or compete to reach their same targets. Try focusing on your strengths and your idea of productivity. When you identify skills you lack or struggle with, you can improve on them.

Keep adapting- Growth comes from perseverance. Try adapting and be open to changing some of your ways. Some ways you adopted at your previous job might not work at your current one, and that is fine. Try to keep an open mind and find things that work for you. Women with ADHD have been naturally finding ways to adapt without realizing it, especially if they were undiagnosed before. Changing your ways may mean you are doing it for the better. Try finding ways that will most suit you and will get the most out of your capabilities.

The Pomodoro technique is a time management tool discovered by Francesco Cirillo in the 1980s. This is used to break down tasks in intervals, typically 25-minute intervals with breaks in between. This uses a kitchen timer shaped like a tomato and was used by the inventor himself as a university student. This method is helpful at work or school. It can also help you make better use of your time and hopefully leave you in a less stressed state and with more free time to spare. The to this technique are as follows:

1.   Chose a task you want to work on. Try to identify how much time it will take you to complete this task. For the sake of using this technique, try to calculate how many Pomodoros are required to complete it, so you must think in blocks of 25 minutes.

2.   Set the timer for 25 minutes. When you set the timer, make sure you do not get distracted, and if need be, set the right work environment before you start the timer.

3.   Work on the chosen task only until the timer is over. This means that no distractions are to be allowed during this time. If you do not manage to do it for the set time, stop the timer and start all over again. If someone distracts you, start over, but ideally, you get to complete your task in a quiet place and let those around you know what you are trying to attain. During this step, you will likely get a better idea of how much time is required to complete that task, especially if you struggle with time management or always seem to have a false sense of time.

4.   Stop working when the timer is up. Try to include reviewing your work during break time to ensure you have completed the task in its entirety. There is also no way of turning the timer back or stopping it before it rings, so you know that if you distract yourself during those 25 minutes, you will not bring back the time you would have wasted on something trivial as opposed to a more important exercise.

5.   If the task you have at hand will not be completed in 25-minutes, divide it into various intervals and try having a short 5-minutes break in between. This will help you distinguish when it is time for work and when you are free to just do whatever you please.

6.   If you have longer tasks that you know will take longer than an hour, give yourself longer breaks. Make sure you identify your goals during your time working. If you want to have better quality or produce more quantity during this time, then make sure this is identified before starting the timer and make sure to keep at it whilst completing the task. This will allow you to dedicate more time to revise your work, for example, if you feel like you need to spend more time on this.

It is very important to follow all steps of this technique; otherwise, it will not be effective. If you did not set your objective and have no specific goal whilst the timer is running, you will likely be unable to complete the task. If you did not get rid of distractions before starting the time, you would very likely have to stop in the middle of it and start over. This will also help you with your estimates and make sure you have more concentration. Because you would have reviewed the task you need to complete and how to reach your goal, you are less likely to have errors, all the while simplifying the process. You will be more likely to be motivated, responsible, and focused when using this technique. Allowing for regular breaks will mean you get to rest or allow yourself to have a treat. This will reduce pressure and tension. You are dividing a bigger goal into much simpler and more structured tasks, so this will help you keep to deadlines, keep you motivated, focused, and almost always ensure success. The task will feel like it is more manageable in this manner.

For women with ADHD, this technique or a similar one that works for them means they will know when to start, and the timer will sort of act as a mini deadline as well, providing enough pressure to stay focused but not too much. The break between intervals will also help you stay motivated. The issue of hyper-focusing will be better managed here because when the time is up, you know you need to stop. This means you will be setting boundaries because your life cannot be overtaken by one task. If you have small tasks that do not require 25 minutes to complete, you can add them up as one task. If you experienced interruptions while the timer was on, it is suggested that you take note of these so you can figure out ways to avoid them during the next cycle. If you manage to finish before the timer, use the remaining time intelligently, and for next time you know how long it takes you to complete that task. Same if you did not manage to complete what you planned in 25-minutes, you know this duty takes more of your time, and you need to dedicate more time to it. In its simplicity, this technique identifies time.

Procrastinating does not mean you are lazy; sometimes it just means you keep putting off tasks to the next day because you do not know where to start, you do not know what it involves to complete, and watching a movie or playing a video game will certainly seem more intriguing. If you need to write an assignment that will require extensive research or a lot of time to write, dividing the task can help you get less disheartened. If you are learning to play a new instrument, try dedicating 25 minutes every day to practice, and you will find that you have made huge progress in a week. 25 minutes a day does not seem a lot out of a 24-hour day, but you can get so much accomplished if you use your time efficiently and effectively. Distractions can be caused by external factors, but most of them are also self-inflicted. Although small distractions may seem insignificant, they do add up at the end of the day. It is not just time you would have wasted but think of how hard it will be to refocus on the task. You may remain distracted and focus on that distraction for over 20-minutes after you have switched off that phone app, and you might still be struggling to regain your concentration. Time may be difficult to understand as it is abstract, but using such techniques can help you change your perception of time, reduce anxiety, and measure your level of productivity. 25-minute intervals are the set target for this technique because people tend to reach their peak for concentration between 25 to 50-minutes with a break that lasts between 5 to 15-minutes. Try performing the tasks you dread the most first. This will keep you motivated because you know far more interesting things await, and the day will get better as it goes by. If your assignments are done on a laptop or computer, try using your break to stay away from monitors. Try not to get off your laptop and move to your phone straightaway during your break. Standing up and moving around will probably benefit you more. You may want to meditate if it is something you like to do or just grab a healthy snack. You may want to set reminders or use functions on your laptop, so you are locked out for the duration of your break; that way, you ensure you take your break and do not hyper-focus.

It is important to realize that multitasking will get you to start on multiple projects and never finish any of them, so avoid doing this. This will create a stressful environment and make you feel enslaved whenever you take work home and work overtime to make up for the lost time. Work on one thing at a time, and if 25 minutes is too little for you to complete the tasks you usually have, then extend that time to 45-minutes, for example, and take longer breaks. The concept is ultimately going to be the same.

To recap this chapter, here are the main points discussed:

Always divide bigger projects into smaller tasks and help to complete that task by using a timer. Use visual reminders to help you remember, whether they are on your phone or written down, find whatever works for you. Surround yourself with people you feel comfortable around, as this will help you stay at ease and feel less stress and overwhelm. If you find it hard to sit still, try using fidget toys during meetings, for example. If you struggle with instructions, try paraphrasing to make sure you understood correctly and help translate it into jargon that you can comprehend. Try getting into the habit of using planners and notebooks. If at any point you feel overwhelmed or it just feels too much, learn to stop and take a breather. Just find whatever works for you.

Chapter 22:
Life-management Tools for Women with ADHD

Women with ADHD want to live a more fulfilling life, and they can do so by reducing their ADHD challenges in their daily lives. Medication can help you reduce some of the challenges but only with changes you make yourself will you be able to achieve a more satisfying life. Therapy can also help you build a life that is more ADHD-friendly. Increasing your knowledge and surrounding yourself with the right people can do magic for you.

You can try the following tools:-

Join a support group- You might have already realized by now that the expectations imposed on you as a woman by society carry a heavier load than you can imagine. With the help of others, it is easier to break free from those unrealistic expectations. One can find encouragement and understanding in these groups and help to create a more realistic approach towards life. These women should be on common ground and help each other deal with almost impossible situations in life.

Educate those around you- There is a lot of misconception about ADHD, especially in neurotypical individuals. Parents might compare you to your siblings and question why you are all over the place when your sister is so organized. Your partner might feel upset about a messy house. People may look at you in resentment when your children misbehave in public, and you cannot control them. Your circle of friends may judge you or pass negative comments about your ways if they do not understand where you are coming from. The people around you should be there to support you and help you live your best life. They should not attack you for your struggles. Teach them and explain to them that most of your actions and behaviors are generated from your ADHD. If they do not know, they will not understand. If you are part of a support group, it will be very beneficial to take them to a session. It will be very valuable for them to listen to other people's struggles and how they overcome them. They will feel like they are not alone, and the situation they find themselves in can be resolved and worked around. They can be more understanding of the situation, and together you can work to manage a more harmonious life. While being open at home can help make those around you more aware of your ADHD, be careful at work. Bosses tend to think you have questionable behavior if you say it out loud. So, at work, try controlling your symptoms of ADHD and outline your strengths and how you reach goals because the way you reach goals is different than neurotypical brains but indistinguishable.

Create an ADHD-friendly environment- If you are a mother with ADHD, one of your kids likely has it too because it is hereditary. It is best to treat your condition and that of other family members with acceptance, and the likelihood of emotional outbursts will decrease. You will be able to reserve your energy for the more positive things in life. You can start by identifying what causes stress around the house and try to eliminate these things. Routines can work great for both parents and children. You know what to expect and what is coming next and so do your kids. This will help them stick to the house rules and leave you feeling less frustrated. Try creating an area where any of you can go to seek shelter when you are exploding with emotions. For kids, it can be a corner of the house with their favorite fidget toys. For an adult, a study room where you can meditate, practice yoga, read a book, or listen to relaxing music can work better. Rather than blaming each other, try resolving the issue. Blame will cause guilt, and you struggle with this already as it is. Problem-solving is not a straightforward process, but it can get easier. If you feel like you lack certain skills or feel like your partner can do certain tasks better, do not be afraid to delegate tasks. The same goes for your children. If you are a mother of two children, one of whom has ADHD, try delegating tasks according to their strengths. This will help put a positive light on their qualities and not exacerbate their flaws. Setting an ADHD-friendly environment needs to apply to all family members irrelevant if they have ADHD or not, it will benefit everyone. Try sorting dirty laundry before washing them. This way, laundry will be less daunting. Have a key hook installed next to the door, so you stop looking for those keys every time! If you often run out of essential items at home like shampoo or laundry soap, try stocking up and keep extras around the house. If you misplace your utensils, try having doubles of the items you often misplace. This will save you the frustration of looking for them and having to find alternatives that don't always work for you. If you are struggling with these tips, try working with a professional ADHD organizer who can help you create an ADHD-friendly home.

Make life easier- Because of societal expectations, women are overbooked already. If you are a woman with ADHD, it is very likely you already struggle with this. Do not be afraid to refuse to take any more commitments. Some tend to not only pack their schedule but that of their children as well. Running from school to private lessons, piano classes, baseball practice, and homework leave children and parents alike drained. Do not forget that wherever your children are scheduled to go, you need to take them. This is on top of your career and house chores. Try to be realistic and keep track of time. You are not robbing your children of their childhood if you do not overpack their schedule as other parents might do.

Exercise regularly- Exercise greatly improves brain function. You do not have to enroll in a state-of-the-art gym or pay for expensive classes. A simple 30-minute home workout can be enough if you add it to your routine. You do not have to work out for hours. 30-minutes, ideally in the morning, is enough. It can be difficult to fit this into your daily routine, but be realistic with yourself and admit that you spend more than 30-minutes on your phone. Try to use your time wisely and stick to 30 minutes of exercise, be it meditation, aerobics, yoga, or any physical activity first thing in the morning because many things can happen during the day that will have you put off exercise every day. If you create a routine, morning activity can get consistent. This will help you focus better during the day and sleep better at night.

Surround yourself with positive vibes- If you are following these tips, you should have educated the people around you about your ADHD. Not everyone can come around to support you and understand where you are coming from. If you feel like your people do not appreciate you and do not bring out the best in you, try changing your clique. When joining a woman support group, you are very much likely to meet people who share your same struggles and will understand you better. Do not compare yourself to others and their perfectionism.

Make time for breathers- Breathers are great for reducing stress. Try compromising with your partner so they can take care of the kids for an hour or so. If your partner is not available, try hiring a babysitter. Make this a ritual, and make sure you do this regularly. Use this time to do whatever you like doing, whatever relaxes you, or simply do nothing. You can take your kids to their grandparents, aunties, or cousins. They keep good contact with their extended family members while you retain your sanity.

Do not exhaust yourself- With managing a house, family, having kids with ADHD, and a career, know that you are already doing your best. You strive to manage your ADHD at work, at home, and with your family, neglecting yourself along the way. Learn to say no and limit your responsibilities. Leave time for yourself.

Appoint or eliminate- Try to identify your strengths, and if you feel that your struggle to accomplish some things, do not be afraid to delegate. If you think you will be better off without a particular commitment in your life, eliminate it. If you also have kids with ADHD, try delegating tasks to them according to their capabilities. If you know one struggles with organizing, assign them a different task they can do better. This will only build their confidence in themselves but will make them feel like they are useful and are just as capable of completing tasks assigned to them. If you struggle to keep the house clean and can afford to hire a housekeeper, do not hesitate to do so. And no, you will not come across as incapable of taking care of your home, but rather create a less stressful environment that all your family will benefit from, including yourself.

Set goals to achieve- One of the hardest things for adults with ADHD is reaching their goals. Planning for people with ADHD can be a struggle, which means we will start working on multiple projects only to finish none. The best way to achieve this is by first choosing a goal and determine what you expect to attain if you reach this goal. Once you have picked a goal, think of how important it is to get to this goal. Make sure you do not choose this target during a momentary rage, as you will likely run out of motivation very soon. Think of what you need to get to this goal and what it will cost you, be it time, money, or energy. Think of what will happen if you do not achieve this goal, is there anything more important you can dedicate your time and energy to? If you start doubting yourself whether achieving this goal is worth it, you might realize there are more important things you can be working on, or maybe you can amend this target so that it is worth achieving. Try to anticipate what obstacles you might come across and how you will overcome them if you do come across them. This will help you chose the best way to navigate getting to your goal, and by now, if this is not the right time, you may want to put it on pause for some time. If you have convinced yourself this is the right goal you need to be working on and figured out how to overcome obstacles as they come, you will need to start monitoring your progress. It might be difficult for women with ADHD to monitor their progress. You can either appoint someone close to you to help keep you on track or, better yet, hire an ADHD coach.

Use a calendar or a planner- This can be on your phone or a traditional hard-back diary. Some find it easier to have everything on their phones, but others prefer the old way and would rather write it down in a planner. Find whatever you prefer if it works. If you make use of a planner, try having it around the house and position it somewhere you will notice first thing in the morning. Your mind will be set up, and you will be aware of what you have planned for the day. This is also very

158

helpful for your kids with ADHD, as they wake up in the morning, seeing they have a day planned and they know exactly what needs to be done, knowing what activity comes next, hopefully facilitating your life along the way. A whiteboard or notes on the fridge may work magic for kids with ADHD. If you have been recently diagnosed with adult ADHD, try opting for a paper calendar or planner; writing things down is said to help you remember more than putting things on your phone. Your phone is flooded with distractions, apps, and adverts that will leave you scrolling on social media unknowingly. You may choose an electronic calendar or application to go with your physical planner. This will help you better along the way and reinforce the lists on your physical calendar. There are many different formats for calendars and planners; chose the one that is most suitable for you and maybe leaves you with some flexibility as well. Try not to get distracted by the fancy design but make sure it is practical.

Do not strive for perfection- You may find yourself comparing your achievements to others. Try not to do that. Once you have a set list of goals or tasks you wish to achieve, try ticking things off your list even if you feel unaccomplished with what you have achieved. Make sure you have done your best, and if that is the case, you would have likely done your best. Do not compare your product to others because you can be striving for perfection when you know that can be hard to achieve. Doing the task sometimes is enough.

Create a jar of success- This is a psychological method to help you or your kids. You can often get discouraged and feel like you never do enough. Try writing your success stories in short on a piece of paper and putting it into this jar. Every time you or your kids get discouraged, get a piece of paper out of the jar, and that little success story can help you reset to a positive mind frame. This can help kids if they each have their jar, or you can use it for relationships too.

Organize your clutter- If you end up holding on to too many sentimental objects, try minimizing these as much as possible. If you can take a photo of it and trash it, that would be ideal; if not, keep these sentimental objects to a minimum. If you pay bills the old ways and have too many papers to file, try switching to electronic and settle your bills via electronic banking, keep folders in your inbox to file electronic receipts and bills. You can also set reminders on your banking app to settle bills or, even better, create a piggy bank to help save a little every month for your yearly health insurance bill or mortgage. If you are subscribed to multiple monthly magazines or newspapers, try switching to online versions.

Manage your time- Try predicting what time you have to leave home to be on time at work or when meeting friends. Try allocating a little extra time for leaving your car or walking to the restaurant from the train station. Work backward and plan how much time you need to get ready and how long it takes you to get there. Try giving a leeway of 15 extra minutes. Make sure you have multiple clocks around the house, at your desk, and on you. This will keep you aware of the time the whole time. If you do not like timers or stopwatches, try keeping track by listening to your favorite songs; it usually all lasts approximately 3 minutes, so calculate in songs instead of time.

Work on your social skills- Try to wait five seconds before jumping into a conversation to speak your mind. Try maintaining eye contact when someone is talking to you to avoid getting distracted and having your mind trail off. If you said something you should not have, apologize for it and explain that you did not intend to say that, and acknowledge what you said was extra. If someone asks you to do something and you know you will forget, ask them to send you a message or a text so you know you can go back to it and are less likely to forget.

Control your emotions- control your breathing if you feel like your emotions are all over the place. If the situation is too much to handle, go to the restroom or a separate room and take time for yourself. Stop apologizing when you do not have to and learn that not everything is your fault.

Adopt healthy eating habits- Plan your meals ahead of time. You do not need to meal prep a week ahead but make a list of breakfast, lunch, and dinner for 7-days. Make sure you have all the ingredients available and keep this list handy. You are less likely to consume food impulsively, especially if you had a rough day at work. You are less likely to go out of your grocery budget if you have one, and you get to choose your meals according to what you like. If you find it hard to prepare the 7-day meal plan, try creating a bigger list of meals you enjoy and take ideas from there every week. Make a list of the things you always want at home and once you run out, put a tick next to it, so you know what you need to get the next time you go to the supermarket. Have a slow cooker or microwave available for quick and easy meals to fit our busy schedule. If you have limited time or dread preparing meals, pick a time during the week to prepare soups or meals in bulk and freeze them. This way, you can always include soup in your meal-prep weekly plan and know you have that ready for when you get home from work. This will have you use the kitchen fewer times during the week.

Adapt to your ADHD- If you are a night owl, work at night if you can. Your phone won't be ringing, and you can work in peace. Try using blue light for alarm clocks because they tend to wake up your brain. Red or amber put you to sleep. Use a pillbox if you often forget to take your ADHD medication and recharge yourself by calming yourself. If you like everything to go in its place or wish you could keep things where they belong, try getting your daily bag with multiple pockets and zippers. You can start putting things in the same place, and you will get used to where everything goes. If you struggle to choose an outfit in the morning, try preparing ahead of time and plan your outfit the night before. If you often misplace your makeup, try using plastic organizers in your bathroom or on your dresser and keep all your essentials in one place. If you often end up looking for wipes or tissues, stock your car with them. If you have recurrent appointments, you need to set repeated reminders on your phone, and if you need to book ahead, set the reminder ahead of time.

Manage your finances- Automate your payments by creating vaults in your accounts or setting direct debits for monthly bills. Use cheque books stubs; like this, you will have a record of what you paid. Keep a small folder for receipts or re-use an old envelope to store your monthly receipt. If you need to budget, you know how much you have spent, and if you need to return an item, you know where to find the receipt. If you prefer keeping hard copies for receipts and bills, try color-coding your folders.

Try not to define yourself by your deficiencies but focus on your talents and strengths. Do not compare to someone else's benchmark. In some ways, ADHD can be a blessing, so celebrate it. Women with ADHD are creative, warm, empathetic, sensitive, humorous, and spontaneous. Try to create an environment where your personality traits are appreciated and given importance.

Chapter 23:
How Exercise can help women with ADHD

ADHD is caused by a malfunction of the brain's attention structure, which is made up of an interconnected network of neurons distributed across different areas of the brain, including those that regulate arousal, motivation, and reward, as well as those that control executive function and movement. Neurotransmitters like norepinephrine and dopamine help usher signals through these attention circuits, and here is where women with ADHD struggle. Treatment for adult ADHD can vary from medication to therapy. This will help regulate the chemical misbalance in the brain. Physical activity is a non-prescription treatment that will help you adjust the chemical composition in your brain. Exercise is often perceived as a way to reduce your waistline and weight. It turns out that exercise can also help shape your brain. During exercise, your brain releases serotonin, dopamine, and norepinephrine. These are the chemicals in your brain that are usually lacking if you have ADHD. Exercise can also decrease the level of adrenaline and cortisol, two chemicals that contribute to your body's level of stress. Physical activity also stimulates the production of endorphins, acts as a mood elevator, and a natural pain killer in the body. Serotonin also helps with depression, mood, and appetite regulation.

Exercising for 30 to 45 minutes a day, three times a week, can help advance cognitive function and behavior. With the release of neurotransmitters in the brain, you are less likely to struggle with going to bed that night, and that feel-good feeling is experienced immediately after you exercise. It usually lasts for about 2 to 3-hours. You are less likely to experience stress during that day or let stress get to you as you usually do when you do not exercise. This is a short-term benefit one experiences with regular exercise. In the long term, regular exercise helps promote neurogenesis, which is the production of new brain cells. Chronic stress and aging can cause a decreased production of neuronal production, so exercise can help combat that.

You might think finding 30 minutes during the day to exercise sounds easier than it is. Some find exercising in the morning far more beneficial for them because they get it out of the way, and the boost they get from exercising will get them ahead in the morning. Others may feel better running after work to clear their minds and help them fall asleep faster. Some may struggle with picking an exercise they enjoy doing in the first place. Ideally, physical activity is done outside because it will reduce symptoms of ADHD even more. Sunlight is also a mood booster. When exercising outdoors, you are likely to be drawn by the sounds and sights around you, pulling your thoughts away from your problems. This can recharge your brain and refresh you. This can be far less boring than running on a treadmill. But if you cannot exercise outside, that is fine. Try picking an activity that works for you and enjoy doing. If you do not like running or walking, try trekking or biking. If you are into video games and find it very hard to get out of your room, then try playing video games that require you to move around.

When creating an exercise program that works for you, you must consider the features of an ADHD brain. ADHD brains need structure, so it is ideal to have structured workouts incorporated into your daily routine. Having someone to overlook your progress like a coach is perfect. ADHD brains seek variety; therefore, you need to allow variety in your exercise program and switch between functional movements, resistance training, and cardiovascular training. Incorporating new functional movements will also help you learn new skills. An ADHD brain usually always works better when there is a set deadline, so you need to set a specific goal to work toward. It can be running a 10K run or simply reduce your stress.

If you want to try the benefits of exercise on your ADHD, follow these strategies to help you incorporate it into your schedule:

Be Accountable- If you set yourself up for home workouts, it is very likely for you to get discouraged easily, and because you do not have to answer to anyone, you are very likely to miss your workout or put it off for the next day. Try choosing an activity that requires a partner, like tennis, squash, running with a friend, making regular appointments with friends at the gym, or booking for classes. This way, you will have a bigger commitment you feel like you need to honor more often. Having a coach or a private instructor will probably make it easier for you if it is something you can afford to do, but it isn't a necessity. The bottom line is that peer pressure is beneficial when considering exercise for an ADHD brain.

Be prepared- If waking up in the morning is already a challenge for you because of your restless nights, try preparing your gym bag the night before, lay out your clothes for the run ahead of time, or book the squash court beforehand. Make it easier for you to go and harder for you to cancel; this way, you are less likely to refuse to stick to your exercise regime.

Be creative- You may get bored easily if all you do is structured and tedious. If you are only motivated after you have new gym wear available, then go and buy some. If you like hiking, try experimenting with different trails and if you like running, try taking different routes. Do not limit yourself to one physical activity because you are more likely to be putting it off every time you must do it. Try having a variety of activities like cycling, running, and squash. If the court is booked or you do not feel like running today, you know you have other things to turn to, and there are no excuses. If there is a new fitness craze like aerial yoga, trampoline workouts, or spinning classes, do not hold back and try them. Physical activity does not have to be boring and repetitive. You are less likely to quit if you vary your exercise regime. Now certain exercises are more beneficial than others, especially for women with ADHD. If you want to get the maximum benefit from your physical routine, ideally, you include circuit, strength, or endurance training. But if you are not a fan, you can still work out; the slightest physical activity will be much more beneficial than doing nothing at all. If you feel like skipping it today, try to anticipate its benefits and the way you feel after doing it; that can help you not postpone.

Take it easy at first- I hope reading this made you excited enough to want to start exercising straight away but start slowly. You do not have to attend the first HIIT class tomorrow morning. Start by walking for 30-minutes daily and increase that as you go along. You may make use of mobile applications to help you increase your endurance or distance over time. Make sure that your plan is sustainable. You do not want to start with too much energy and burn out shortly after. It can be tempting to overdo it at first because you may hyper-focus on the benefits of this, it is a new thing in your life, and you want to yield those benefits. You can create a simple circuit training set including push-ups, squats, use homemade weights, or your body weight.

Set a routine-Try exercising at the same time every day. Mornings are ideal for some, but it isn't a set rule. You need to make adaptations according to your errands, family commitments, and work schedule. Getting exercise done first thing in the morning can help you get it out of the way straight away, and you can be less likely to postpone it as if you had it scheduled later during the day. If you work a 9 to 5 job, working out before going to work can be very beneficial, especially if you have meetings first thing in the morning. The neurotransmitter boost you get from exercising can last for approximately 3 hours, and this can cover a portion of your shift at work. It can help you stay focused during meetings and gets you to concentrate on clearing that inbox in the morning. This can have you less panicked and stressed during the day because it can seem like you have less clutter. You may want to start with the more difficult tasks in the morning because this chemical boost will help you get those things done quicker without nagging doing them in the first place.

Compensate yourself- Cut yourself some slack and reward yourself after you manage to work out. If you find running on a treadmill at the gym boring, try making a playlist specifically for when you are running at the gym. Select tracks that you enjoy listening to and can keep you motivated. If you like smoothies or shakes, make sure you award yourself with one after your workout is complete. Do give yourself credit for actually completing a task. It may seem trivial for an athlete to incorporate exercise in their lifestyle, but it is a struggle for you, and that is fine. You may snack on your favorite refreshment once you have completed your physical program because you deserve it.

Record your activity- If your target is to improve symptoms of ADHD, you do not have to weigh yourself every morning. You need to record what you did for physical activity on that day, for how long, and how you felt after it was over. If you postponed it or canceled your plans, keep a record of it just the same and make sure you take note of why this happened. If this happens often and is always because of the same reason, you can know what is getting in your way. If the time you selected for exercising is getting you late to work, then you know you must change your schedule or exercise at a different time. This should not have you blaming yourself for not exercising but rather help eliminate whatever is getting in the way of achieving your goals. Find specific goals and what you hope to attain by exercising regularly. If you are focusing on reducing stress and increasing focus, take into consideration whether you are reaching your goals with your current physical activity plan and tweak it as required.

Make it accessible- Driving to the gym every morning can make you feel disheartened. If you live in an urban area, trekking may be impractical because you must drive to start your trail. Try investing in cheap home equipment and dedicating a corner of your house to it. This way, you can wake up in the morning and work out, or if you feel a boost of energy, you do not have to physically get ready and be somewhere. If you suffer from impulsivity, this might be very beneficial for you to use up the excess energy you might have. The easier it is to access your exercise program, the more likely you are to stick with it and be consistent. Do not let things get in between your goals.

Find your power source- Your goal is not losing weight here but making sure your ADHD symptoms are controlled and you should be motivated to keep going. The scope of this is to treat your mind and manage your symptoms. Recording your activity can help you monitor how you feel and when you see that you are reaping the results for it, you are more likely to keep doing what you are doing.

It is best to consult your doctor before starting an exercise regime, especially if you suffer from any other chronic conditions or are pregnant. Exercise is a free and fun way of controlling your ADHD. You need to understand the benefits of exercise to convince yourself to get started and get over that initial hurdle. From walking your dog to dancing, you can find ways to exercise unknowingly if the idea of sticking to an exercise regime sounds hideous to you. If you feel like going for a walk is boring, try listening to your favorite podcast while you do so. Fitness can ease your stress and anxiety levels and enhance your working memory. It can improve your impulse control and decrease compulsivity. Exercise can help you improve executive function, something you already struggle with. Because women with ADHD tend to be more impulsive and binge eat under stress, exercise will help them maintain a healthy weight. This will consequently reduce your risk of heart-related diseases and diabetes. Fitness enables you to control your blood pressure levels and cholesterol levels. It also helps with strengthening your bones and improve overall mood and self-esteem. Making treatment choices can be complicated, as many adults with ADHD know. Prescription drugs, on the one hand, can help with symptoms, but they will not magically solve any of your problems immediately. Even if the medication is working, you can still experience forgetfulness, emotional issues, social ineptitude, and you may experience disorganization, distractibility, and relationship issues. It is important to note, though, that medication is not the only choice for treating ADHD. Experts now agree that daily exercise is one of the most important things you can do for your health. Scientists have discovered that moderate exercise causes changes in many of the same neurochemicals and brain structures as common ADHD drugs do.

Hyperactivity has also been linked to an overactive cerebellum, which is an area of the brain located at the back. This is responsible for receiving information from the sensory system and regulating motor activity. It also helps voluntary coordination movement, including balance, posture, and speech. ADHD drugs elevate dopamine levels and norepinephrine to bring this area of the brain back to normal. Exercise has also been shown to mimic the same function of ADHD medication in this area. This is where neurogenesis happens, as referenced earlier. People who exercise regularly will dramatically improve their levels of brain-derived neurotrophic factor, also known as BDNF and referenced as neurogenesis. This growth takes place in the cerebellum.

Does it mean that if you manage to stick to a regular and effective exercise program, you can stop taking your medication? No. As previously mentioned, ADHD is a spectrum, so severity can vary. Some women can find exercise to be a replacement for prescription drugs because they usually experience mild to moderate symptoms. If you are already on medication, it does not mean that exercise will not benefit you. Physical activity needs to be complementary to your treatment. It will help increase attention and improve your mood. After consulting with your doctor, you may want to adjust the timings for your medication. If you exercise in the morning, for example, you may delay taking your stimulant medication 3 hours after your workout, so you can benefit from the cognitive boost produced by exercise. You are more likely to be less hyperactive after exercising, and you will have more mental clarity.

Just know that exercise and ADHD are a winning pair. ADHD brains work better after a good exercise.

Chapter 24:
6 Executive Function Strategies that Really Work for People with ADHD

E xecutive functions are a set of processes used to manage oneself and one's resources to reach a goal. This involves neurologically-based skills like mental control and self-regulation. Depending on your ADHD severity, this can mean that life is a little bit harder to manage or feels completely unmanageable. People who lack executive function may struggle to plan their day, remember things that have been told to them, or get things done on time. The pre-frontal cortex is the part of the brain assigned to control our executive function, and this area of the body is still developing till age 25. It is proved that people with ADHD have a 30% delay in this area of the brain. Although not everyone with ADHD will struggle in the same way, people with ADHD have some sort of overall impairment. They are often perceived to be lazy and exhibit a lack of effort or seem childish.

Before getting to the strategies that can help executive dysfunction, it is best if one can understand the areas that are affected by our executive functions:

1. **Initiation-** One can struggle to start projects or tasks out of their own free will. They struggle to come up with problem-solving ideas and often procrastinate working on tasks they know well need to be done. You might wait for someone else to start something and then join them to contribute.

2. **Inhibition-** One may struggle to stop certain behavior at an appropriate time and can have a hard time not acting out in certain situations. They can often come across as impulsive and behave inappropriately in some situations.

3. **Emotional control-** One can struggle managing emotions and may respond to certain situations inappropriately in the eyes of those around them. One may lash out in anger before even giving time to the other person to voice their opinion. There would be no break in between emotions and what is said, literally like speaking their mind.

4. **Shift-** One may struggle with transitioning from one task to the next and often dislike when things do not go as planned. They struggle with being flexible, and if they are asked to do something they were not prepared to do, they may struggle with shifting their attention and energy to it. People with executive dysfunction would rather stick to their schedule and have a hard time moving from one activity to another without getting distracted or lost.

5. **Working memory-** People with executive dysfunction may struggle with holding information long enough to complete the task at hand. It can be difficult to take notes during class or a meeting, for example, to go back to that information later.

6. **Planning and organization-** Someone with executive dysfunction may struggle to manage current or future plans. Planning an event or a holiday can be difficult because there are

many steps involved, and one must get organized to complete a plan on time.

7. **Organizing materials-** It can be tough keeping things in order if you have executive dysfunction and may struggle to retrieve your stuff when you need them. You may have a cluttered home or a disorganized station at work.

8. **Self-Monitoring-** Because you struggle with impulsivity and organization, it is very difficult to recognize how you treat those around you. It is difficult to track our flaws and work towards fixing them.

If you have a relative or close friend who you know struggles with executive functions, it is best to ask them in which areas they struggle most and how it affects them personally. If you are someone suffering from executive dysfunction, there are some behavioral tasks that you can make habits that will help with this:

- Make use of organizers, lists, planners, alarms, and reminders! Use anything that can help you remember.

- Ask for written instructions, whether it is in a meeting or something your partner wants to be done in the house. These instructions will help you remember and facilitate the process of completing the tasks as you should. It is a fact that people with ADHD will struggle with functioning memory so writing things down is key.

- Plan your day and make sure you have a schedule set up. If you need to set alarms or reminders so they can alert you to check your schedule and go by it, do so.

- Try to break down large tasks into smaller ones. Because people with executive dysfunction can have a hard time dealing with large goals, distributing the tasks into smaller ones can make it easier to complete and will give you a better understanding of the time it takes for you to complete each task. Make sure that each deadline is written down and is clear. Whenever you are working on each task, make sure that the deadline is visible to make sure you do not miss out on completing tasks on time.

- Make sure you have separate spaces for leisure and work. It is easier to concentrate and get straight to work if you have a designated work area and you do not have to work in bed, for example. You are less likely to be productive if your brain is used to relaxing on the couch or in bed, and you also use that area to work.

- Set reminders to prepare yourself for transitions. If you struggle to switch from task to task, make sure you allow yourself a few minutes before switching from one task to the next. If you need to conduct a presentation at work, make sure you set a timer 5 minutes before the presentation to go in there with the right mindset. Unfortunately, this is not something that can be applied to all situations in life as some things happen unexpectedly, and there would be no other option but to adapt and carry on, but wherever possible, allow yourself some time to get ready for your next task. This will reduce further disappointment and stress.

- Allow time to think before interacting with others. Because someone with executive dysfunction tends to be impulsive, it is best to think before expressing our emotions or speaking our minds. We might say things we did not intend to or that we maybe should not have said. Remember, things you say cannot be taken back. This will save you embarrassment and avoid hurting others as well. Not everyone knows you may do this unintentionally.

If the above advice was given to you plenty of times before and you just feel like you simply cannot follow through with these habits, then the following six Executive Function Strategies that really Work for People with ADHD should be a blessing:

1. "Out of sight is out of mind"- *John Heywood's 1546*

    People with ADHD tend to live by this saying unknowingly. Storing things on top of each other can cause clutter and can be difficult if you are looking for something. Try storing things vertically so you can see all the items. It is best if you make use of clear containers to store your items as well, from jeans to shirts and spices in the kitchen. This will help you stay organized and makes sure that all things are visible.

2. Make use of bullet journals. Most planners and calendars are designed for neurotypical brains, and people with ADHD can start off using a standard planner only to disregard it a few

weeks after. There are plenty of ways to design a bullet journal specifically targeted at people with ADHD. Ideally, it would have flexibility so you can design as you please. Too much design can often distract you from the main purpose of this, staying organized and sticking to deadlines. Writing things physically can help you remember tasks and deadlines more than if you had to use an electronic app for the same functions. Having electronic planners or calendars means you are more likely to get distracted by adverts, pop-ups, or find yourself on social media unknowingly. Bullet journals have the flexibility of a regular notebook but are also structured as a regular planner. You can create a key, an index, including daily, monthly, and weekly logs, plus you are free to tailor it to your needs. You may create one by simply using an empty notebook and a pen. The idea of a bullet journal was created to give people, specifically those with ADHD, the flexibility they need but keep them grounded. Unfortunately, in today's world, one might still fall for an electronic calendar because if you are scheduling meetings with others, there is no way for them to know what you have written down in your journal. Ryder Carroll, an ADHD himself, has created this journal and confirms using this journal to empty your mind and write down everything you intend to do during the day, week, or month. The monthly planners can still be used even if you still use an electronic calendar. You may want to list down all the things you intend to do and then find a place for each of them in your electronic planner. You can keep track of your previous month and evaluate how much you have achieved, what you have missed doing, and why. If you have taken on too much that month, you can take up fewer responsibilities the following month. If your planning did not work well, you can find and fix the flaws for the coming months. Often, people with ADHD can struggle with the guilt and shame of not completing tasks as if this makes up for what you missed out on doing. The bullet journal will help you improve on these skills and allow you to appreciate the effort and the work you have done by focusing on all the tasks you have completed. Setting reminders to check your journal is perfectly fine and suggested for people with ADHD. If you wish to keep one journal to have everything in one place rather than having information scattered on different notebooks in your car, at the office, and in your house, you may do so, so using an app for temporary thoughts, ideas, or appointments when your journal is not handy, is fine too. Set reminders to jot updates on the original journal so you can have everything in one place and information is updated. Put challenging things on top of your to-do list so you will get it over and done at the start of your day, and everything else that follows during the day will seem less hard to complete. Creating a key for your journal will help you create symbols that work magic for speedy ADHD brains. Put page numbers in your notebook because you will need to update your index as you go. No more forgotten post-it notes or little misplaced pieces of paper. You can also include a future log that means you can jot everything you want to include later but can avoid worrying about it for now. If you are the artistic type and use your notebook to sketch or draw, you can do so here as well if you add it to your index. You know what pages you have reserved for drawing, and you can go back to them if you want to. You can briefly plan your months in the monthly log and go into further detail in the daily logs. You can leave one page for a brief plan of your day to keep you updated on what is to come on that day. The opposite page can be used to go into further detail as to what is required to complete your plan for the day; if you need supplies for that meeting or if you need to go to the grocery store, you may include the shopping list also. The detailed daily log is there to help you remember what you need to complete your tasks, but if you do not want to feel overwhelmed in the morning when you look at the planner, you may want to only consider looking at the summarized version. This will keep you on track but still have the detailed version as a backup to help you remember. Because you can migrate tasks from one month to the next, this can help you prioritize important duties and make you realize that the task you have putting off and postponing for months now may not be as important. If you keep on postponing tasks from one month to the next, you can realize that you cannot keep on doing this, and you cannot magically get a thousand things done next month.

3. If you struggle with initiation because you tend to procrastinate, try meeting with a friend in a coffee shop or at each other's house and plan to work on things you need to get done. Make sure you make it clear that this is not a coffee date, but you need that little spark to start working on your duties because otherwise, you will never get them done.

4. When you have big projects to complete against a deadline, do not feel like you are putting it off because you are lazy. ADHD brains are wired to think that most tasks are far more difficult than they are, and that is why they procrastinate. Tell your mind that you do not have to start working on the entire project but only start working on a small portion of it. If you manage to convince yourself that starting little by little is enough, before you know it, you would be getting on with more than just a minor part of the task. Remember that ADHD brains tend to hyper-focus but getting starting is more difficult. So, initiation can be the biggest hurdle. You are very likely to persevere at this project after you have started working on it. If you are dividing larger projects into smaller ones, this step is useful for each step. Make sure you understand the benefits of initiation and why getting yourself to start slowly will ultimately lead you to complete the task eventually. If you do not feel like working on this project at any given time, try to give yourself a break and avoid judging yourself, but know that this is the only stumbling block you will encounter along the way.

5. If you have been told that you are too emotional or too loud, that is because those around you focus more on emotional control. You would rather feel emotions deeply and express them without boundaries if you have ADHD. What you need to take as advice is therapy by professionals; give yourself the love and care that you need. Create boundaries and accept only the treatment you deserve. You have the freedom to occupy space in the universe.

6. Outsource duties that you cannot do yourself. Do not persist in completing tasks that are not important to you or tasks you are not good at. As a kid, you might have been pushed to read for subjects or credits in school you were not keen on doing because they were part of the curriculum, but as an adult, you have the freedom to choose your career and only do things you love to do. If you are delegating chores at home because your partner mutually agrees to it and supports your ADHD, then you are already doing this. You might be doing this unknowingly; if you hire someone to service your car or get a housekeeper weekly to help you tidy up. If you spend your time struggling to complete tasks you are not good at, that is only taking precious time away that can be used on things you enjoy doing, are good at, and highlight your potential rather than putting you down.

Incorporating the tips and skills mentioned above can help get a better hold on your life and manage your ADHD better. Change can take time to adapt to, and that is understandable. Know the benefits of change and recognize you are giving it your all.

Chapter 25:
The 15 most effective methods for coping with ADHD

S ymptoms of ADHD can easily interrupt your day-to-day activities. Fortunately, there are a variety of approaches you can take to effectively handle your condition and treat your symptoms. These will help you live in harmony and manage your condition better.

Try the below methods to help you cope with ADHD:

1. Get Diagnosed

   If you suspect having ADHD, make getting a diagnosis a priority. The scope of this is not to have you labeled but getting you diagnosed can have a positive impact on how you perceive yourself. You are more likely to forgive yourself for the shortcomings you had in the past and have more control over your current life. There is a condition for what you are going through, and getting diagnosed can give you a sense of relief. It is not a death sentence to have ADHD; it is a result of the way the brain is wired, and understanding how it works can help you lead a better life.

2. Make self-care a habitude!

   If you have ADHD, you probably hyper-focused to a point where you forgot to eat, sleep, or use the restroom. Try checking in on yourself occasionally. It is accepted to work on the task for a long time because it needs to be finished, but if you know this can happen, try keeping snacks on your desk for when you get hungry. Make frequent visits to the grocery shop and make sure you opt for healthy snacks and not junk food. Try getting up in the morning and getting ready for a day's work by having a shower and make yourself breakfast, even if you are working from home. Start by decluttering your space and consider making your bed every morning even though you are not expecting anyone to come over. If you manage your health, then managing everything else just follows.

3. Get a healthy amount of sleep!

If you are restless, you are more likely to have exacerbated ADHD symptoms. This can affect your attention span, memory, and problem-solving skills. Issues with sleep issues is a common problem you might face, and the cure can be as simple as a change of habit. If you are getting less sleep than you need, you are likely to be more irritable. Adding physical activity can help you get a restful night.

4. Identify conditions arising from ADHD.

ADHD rarely exists on its own. If you have ADHD, you are very likely to have one or more other conditions. This should not be an alarming discovery, but rather, the goal is to raise awareness. If you are a woman with undiagnosed or misdiagnosed ADHD, you probably have already been diagnosed with these coexisting conditions before being diagnosed with ADHD itself. Identify what coexisting conditions you have and start treating each one directly. Sometimes symptoms of coexisting conditions can be disguised by symptoms of ADHD or the other way round. Other conditions coexisting with ADHD can be anxiety disorders, bipolar disorder, depression, personality disorders, and substance use disorders. It is crucial to share all symptoms with your physician when discussing your ADHD symptoms as well. This can help your physician get a full diagnosis and give you the treatment you need.

5. Drive carefully.

Women with ADHD tend to feel very distracted and inattentive when driving. You can increase safety on the roads by opting for a manual transmission instead of an automatic one. This can help you become more engaged while driving, and you are less likely to switch your attention to something else other than driving. Try switching off your phone before you start driving and avoid using a headset. If music distracts you, remove your stereo system. Do not do recreational drugs and use alcohol before driving, as these can reduce your focus even more.

6. Give up perfectionism!

You do not need to be perfect. You probably spend too much time on trivial things, and this is detrimental to your health. Perfecting small things takes time away from more important tasks leaving you working on the bigger, most important tasks under further stress and anxiety. This can have you missing deadlines of far more crucial things.

7. Learn the art of time management!

   If you are a woman with ADHD, you probably struggle with time management. You often miss deadlines and underestimate the power of time. You may struggle to anticipate how much time a task can take you to complete. If you also hyper-focus, you may devote your time and energy to one task leaving others undone. This can leave you feeling stressed and overwhelmed. Create a schedule and get organized. Try writing down the things you want to get done the night before and prioritize your list. Do consider your strengths and not only your weaknesses. This will boost your self-esteem and confidence. If you start working on a task or plan to, allow some extra time than you anticipate it will take. This can help you manage your time better and leave you with fewer disappointments. Make use of timers or alarms; this way, you know for how long you need to work on a particular task whether you like doing it or not.

8. Physical activity

   If you have the hyperactive type of ADHD, you may highly benefit from this. Either way, exercise can help you focused and calm. Physical activity is not only great for your health but also for your mind. This can help you channel your energy in the right way and can help you rest better at night.

9. Make use of pillboxes.

   If you are a woman with ADHD one medication, you may struggle to remember whether you have taken your medication or remembering to take it at all. Using a pillbox can help you stay alert for when your medication is running low because you would prepare a week's supply in advance. This can help you manage your filling of prescriptions better and avoid leaving you without treatment for some time. This can save you from carrying multiple boxes with you wherever you go. A pillbox can also keep you more organized, and if you forgot whether you have taken it or not, all you need to do is look back in your pillbox. There are pillboxes with timers within them if you feel like you have enough reminders on your phone.

10. Learn to say no!

Women with ADHD tend to be people-pleasers and often feel anxious when saying no. Do not take more than you can handle as this can only leave you overwhelmed, stressed, and anxious. If you want to help, try taking on tasks you know you enjoy and can complete. If you are asked to participate or commit, do not say yes straight away but postpone it and say you will think about it. If you commit as soon as you are asked, you are likely to say yes involuntarily, whereas if you give it some thought, you can make a more informed decision and only take on tasks you really want to.

11. Keep a clock in your shower.

You may not admit it, but you spend more time in your bathroom than you should. You can get carried away wondering about your next invention, things you should have said, or things you have done in the past when under the shower. Keep a clock in your bathroom to help you stay on top of time and avoid getting carried away by unnecessary thoughts.

12. Look for help!

It is perfectly fine to ask for help. If you feel you are struggling at any given task, do not be afraid to ask for help, email your superior for further instructions via email about that project, and if you are struggling in life in general, do not be afraid to seek help from a therapist if you feel like you need a little extra help together with your medication.

13. Create a master list.

You can use this in addition to your bullet journal or your favorite mobile application. Make a list of whatever comes to mind, and make sure you always have a notebook handy. Handling this master list can be a little overwhelming, so it is suggested that this is done in combinations with a planner. You can take items from the master list and jot them down on your planner in order of prioritization. This can help you plan your day better with tasks you actually intended to complete at some point.

14. Monitor your impulsive behavior.

You probably struggled at some point with impulse buying or binge eating. Try to go for healthier stimulations like music, exercise, puzzles, fidget toys, or just a good laugh with a friend. Avoid falling for substance abuse and alcohol consumption; if you struggle to control your impulses, especially when it often drives you to the latter, try getting professional help.

15. Consult with an ADHD-oriented nutritionist.

Numerous studies have shown that artificial flavors, colors, and other ingredients can lead to increased feelings of violence and hyperactivity. Eat nutritious meals and snacks during the day and avoid candy and yeast goods. With the help of a nutritionist, you can plan your meals better, prepare a grocery shopping list ahead of time, and help you have healthy food available all the time. Sticking to a list of healthy items can help you spend much less time wandering at the supermarket and can almost guarantee you will walk out with everything you need without having to go back immediately because you missed an important item on the list. A nutritionist that understands or has worked with people with ADHD can help keep you accountable.

Some things are easier said than done! Knowing where to begin and what methods you need to apply to get better is what you need to start your journey towards a better-navigated life with ADHD.

Chapter 26:
How to stop losing things

P eople with ADHD constantly lose or misplace things. This is because you are distracted when putting things away and cannot recollect the last place you left them. You may put things down for what seems to be a split of a second and forget about where you left it. When looking for that thing you just misplaced, you are very likely to get distracted by external stimuli, like the sound coming from your TV set or that open videogame on your laptop. You can empty the dishwasher and do a full load of laundry before remembering to start looking for that thing you lost 2 hours ago. This can cause most people with ADHD to be often late to work or meeting with friends. Some people with ADHD tend to compensate for this inner turmoil and end up being extremely organized, almost perceived as obsessive-compulsive, but not every ADHD brain is like this.

Try having a dedicated place for everything you use. This strategy can work for the neurotypical brain without struggle, but for an ADHD brain, you might need to modify it a bit to make it suitable for your needs. Putting things away where they mostly make sense does not always work. Something can make sense to be placed somewhere in particular now, but this may not come to mind when you are looking for it. Try placing things where they are most useful. Think of a restaurant or a coffee bar. Every server would have their station, which is always replenished. It does not make sense to have a server cross the opposite side of the restaurant to get a fork because they are very likely to be stopped a million times by people along the way constantly asking for things. Those people in a restaurant are the external stimuli people with ADHD struggle to block out. If you take an umbrella with you before leaving the house, try leaving an umbrella holder near the door. If you often leave your jacket everywhere but where it needs to be, try having a coat hanger next to the door. If you often misplace your keys, try installing a key holder next to your door. Your keys can have multiple points of usage because you can place them in your car, bag, or house. Keep those places to a minimum to avoid confusion whenever you need to go look for them. It is perfectly fine to have duplicates or more copies of one item around the house. Take your phone charger as an example. You will probably need one in the bedroom, one in the living room, and another at your desk. That is fine. You will avoid looking for it every time you need to charge your phone.

Make it easy to put things back because you know you can struggle with this. You can make use of a label machine to label where things go. This can make it easier for you to put things back, and you do not have to remember where everything is meant to go. Placing things in clear containers can help you know what is in them without having to hover down every canister in your house. Make things fun to put back. Decorate your space and make sure you can easily get acquainted with where things should go. Think of it as if it is a puzzle. Spare some time during the day, usually in the morning before you leave the house and, in the evening, before you go to bed and scan for things that are out of place. Have a look around you, and you can probably notice things that are out of place. Take some time to but them back. This can help you keep a decluttered space every day without having a backlog of lost and misplaced items. It can also help you find things easily whenever you need them. Try this with your workstation as well. Try decluttering it every day at the end of your shift. This can help you start the next morning on a good note. Do the same thing with your dishes; try putting dirty dishes in the dishwasher if you have one, or make sure you clean everything after you finish eating. Like this, you can avoid procrastinating and can avoid ending up with a pile of dirty dishes, which you probably put off for days before you get yourself to clear that sink up.

If you are a woman with ADHD who shares a home with a partner who likes to keep things organized, you might have ended up in a fight a couple of times because they misplaced your things in the name of tidying up. Them clearing your space does not necessarily mean they are helping you. You may struggle with finding things you put away, let alone when someone else does that for you. You have a lesser chance of findings things you are looking for when someone clears the space on your behalf. Try to always clear your things yourself, or if anyone else is helping you do that, make sure you agree on where things should go. You can encourage yourself to put things back by making things fancy and as attractive to get your attention as possible, but things will stay put only if they are practical to you. Make things easier to be put back and try to facilitate this process for yourself as much as possible.

Depending on how important that thing you just misplaced is, you are often going to feel anxious, stressed, and annoyed when you lose it. Do your best to be organized; highlight, label, or decorate areas, so they get your attention, and you can misplace things less often. If you often misplace small things like your wedding ring or watch, try keeping them in a bigger container like a bowl as soon as you walk in and out the door. Try to do one thing at a time because it has been established that people with ADHD struggle with multitasking, so this cannot help you find things when you lose them. If you need that set of keys because otherwise you cannot get out the door, try to ignore all other distractions and focus only on finding the keys, try to recall where you placed them last, and go look for them there. If you often misplace your stationery at work or home if you work remotely, try using a compact desk organizer so all your stationery items can stay collected in one place. Try making it a habit to clear your desk and place everything in your drawer before leaving at the end of the shift.

If you often misplace your phone, keys, watch, and tablet, try introducing a docking station in your life. Leave it where you are most likely to leave the items that go on it. You can have all your valuables and electronics in one place and charged at one point. This way, you can lessen the times you walk out of the house with your phone uncharged. The chargers can all be at one place, and as soon as you walk in the house, you know where things have to go because you want them charged by the next morning too. You know where to look for things before walking out of the house as well. You can include compartments in the docking station to host things that do not necessarily need to be charged, like your house keys, your precious bullet journal, and your glasses.

You may find it even harder to find things you do not use often. Say you have many small items you usually always use only for traveling, like your passport, your travel toothbrush, your luggage tag, or your padlocks. Try creating a space around the house that is dedicated to these items only. Keep everything in a visible container and label it or decorate it as you please.

If you wake up in the morning struggling to make a cup of coffee because everything is everywhere, try to create a designated area for coffee-making if this is something you often do and struggle with every day. There are plenty of fancy ideas online that will help you create a coffee station and make it a fun project. Try keeping your favorite mugs, a couple of spoons, coffee machine, tea, coffee, and sugar in one place. The next time you need to make a coffee, it can be a breeze with this strategy.

If you have a project to deliver at work the next morning and need supplies to be taken to work, you can struggle to sleep at night knowing the things you must remember. Avoid the restless night and make a list. Gather all the things you know you will need and place them in your car, in your drive-in, or by the door. Collect everything you need to take with you, and if it helps, try making a list and leaving it where you can see it the next morning. This way, you can check off the things you need to take with you and avoid the anxiety or stress that comes with all of this. Although the last thing you feel like doing after a day at work or running errands is clearing the clutter or organizing your stuff, try making putting things back a habit and part of your routine. It can be difficult until you make this a habit.

Chapter 27:
22 Things not to say to someone with ADHD

I f you, your kids, or your partner have ADHD, you will almost certainly meet skeptics who do not understand the disorder or its implications in daily life. Unfortunately, there are a lot of myths about ADHD, and these misconceptions can be harmful to those that have the disorder. Some people incorrectly label ADHD as a "made up" condition that is over-diagnosed and over-medicated. Others see ADHD as a harmless, insignificant disorder that can be easily handled with good parenting and fades away in adulthood. Whether you have a child with ADHD, a partner with ADHD, or if you have ADHD yourself, you've probably heard any of the following erroneous and upsetting comments about ADHD. It is crucial to know what to avoid saying so that you can be as helpful as possible to people who have ADHD.

If you have ADHD, the following things are the last things you want to hear:

1. ''ADHD is just an excuse to be lazy''- Those around neurodiverse brains tend to visualize the person as the problem rather than recognizing the disorder or the condition as the problem.

2. ''You need to try harder to get organized''- People with ADHD will often struggle to get organized like the neurotypical brains, and they can, in most times, fail to do so successfully. This can make people with ADHD feel like a failure, and although one would try hard enough, they can still come across as not doing enough from someone else's

perspective. People with ADHD must find their way and methods to stay organized because other people's ways will not work for them.

3. "Taking ADHD medication is a bad idea"- Medication is not the only means of treatment for ADHD. You can opt for therapy, supplements, exercise, and neurofeedback. There is no compulsory approach for ADHD, and because it is a spectrum, severity can vary. Treatment for ADHD needs to be adapted to the lifestyle of the ADHD brain and its goals.

4. "Stop Overreacting"- People with ADHD do not overreact, but because of emotional dysregulation, their emotions tend to be heightened.

5. "ADHD is not real; we need to let kids be themselves"- Some people are unaware of the reality of this condition that they do not consider it a real disorder. Some may say you do not allow kids to be energetic and do not allow them to be themselves. Some blame technology because you have set a standard of kids playing on their tablets rather than letting them play outside like old times. If kids who are now adults went undiagnosed or misdiagnosed, it does not mean that ADHD is a modern disorder and did not exist in the past; there was not enough knowledge about it.

6. "Everyone has a little bit of ADHD, or an ADHD moment, it is nothing major"- Anyone can experience occasional moments of forgetfulness or inattentiveness. Some people claim to have had an ADHD moment, which can be normal incidents for neurotypical brains. Little do they realize that ADHDers do not occasionally experience this

but rather find it hard to focus anywhere unless it is something they are super devoted to.

7. "ADHD is diagnosed far too easily and regularly"- To the contrary of this common misconception, ADHD in women is not diagnosed enough. It has been established by now that when compared to boys, girls live much of their life believing they suffer from depression or anxiety if their ADHD has been misdiagnosed.

8. "People use ADHD as an excuse for bad behavior"- People with ADHD may deliver a task on time when it happens to be something that triggers their hyper-focus. They may perform other tasks poorly and will therefore be perceived as inaccurate and unreliable. The neurotypical brains that are not aware of this condition would not understand the impairments associated with ADHD. Really and truly, people with ADHD put a lot of time, effort, and energy into staying on track and just being organized.

9. "That child needs more discipline"- Many parents deal with these statements when out and about with their kids in public. These comments come across as judgments towards their parenting abilities.

10. "ADHD is caused by poor parenting"- Children with ADHD can be more challenging to bring up, but poor parenting skills or lack of control are not the causes of ADHD. It is common practice to blame yourself as a parent when your child is diagnosed, and these delusions certainly do not help. The environment by which the kids surround themselves can impact how ADHD is expressed, but it does not cause it.

11. "Students or employees who obtain special accommodations for ADHD have an unfair advantage."- People with ADHD do not receive special treatment to give them an advantage over others but rather to level the playing field and make it fair for everyone. Remember, people with ADHD will do the same things and achieve the same goals but with different processes.

12. "In females, ADHD is less intense than in males."- This is not the case at all as women with ADHD have symptoms that are overlooked. Because boys would disrupt the classroom and hinder learning for the other students, their behavior must be treated. Girls can often be perceived as disorganized and lazy, and these can only interfere with their learning processes. Girls internalize their symptoms and are at a greater risk of sexual promiscuity, teen pregnancies, alcohol abuse, drug abuse, and cigarette smoking. Because you do not see the symptoms, it does not mean they are not there. Undiagnosed females, like undiagnosed males with ADHD, are at risk for chronic underachievement. The difficulties that ADHD mothers have dealing with the demands of daily life can easily spill over into parenting. Because of the genetic connection between ADHD and parenting, many of these mothers will have children with the disorder, who will need even more organization, focus, and consistency.

13. "Did you take your meds today?"- This is something neurotypical brains would say when they are in a close relationship with someone with ADHD. ADHDers can come across as goofy or too loud at times, and that is probably not attributed to their ADHD or them skipping their medication, but because their character is that way. This can easily translate to someone not liking your character, and they like you better

when you are under the effect of medication. Coming from someone close to you can make it even more offensive because they are the ones that should be the most understanding of your situation.

14. "It is not that hard to focus"- You can never say to someone with a broken leg to walk because it is not that hard for you to do with two fully functioning lower limbs. The same goes for people with ADHD. Where neurotypical brains have no issue blocking external distractions, people with ADHD struggle just to shut off the sound of that ticking clock in the classroom. They process everything around them without filtering the most important things.

15. "Calm down"- Because of emotional dysregulation, people with ADHD can seem over-excited in certain situations, and those around them may want to quiet them down. Ideally, ADHDers are left to express themselves in whatever way they deem fit. In the case of kids, if they need to be told to calm down, ideally, this is to be done discretely, and the reason behind their excitement and why it is inappropriate in that situation should be explained. In general, whether someone has ADHD or not, telling them to calm down can guarantee they won't calm down. Try telling that to your angry partner and see where it takes you!

16. "My boyfriend's brother's friend from high school has ADHD, I understand"- ADHD severity varies from person to person, and no two people with ADHD are the same. Because you know someone, or you met someone you know has ADHD once does not make you universally understand every other ADHD person. Try to be more considerate towards that individual as a person and do not compare them to others.

199

17. "How you could forget that"- If you mentioned something to a neurodiverse individual and they seem to not have a clue that this even happened, keep in mind that they might have been toppled by a million distractions. The last thing they need is being judged for something they forgot to remember.

18. "I think I have ADHD too"- Everyone can experience a little forgetfulness or inattention now and again, but self-diagnosis is not acceptable here. People with ADHD go through multiple tests and evaluations to get hold of their diagnosis. This can also be why everyone underestimates the severity of ADHD and can struggle to understand a neurodiverse brain.

19. "You can't have ADHD, you are too smart"- ADHD does not affect your intelligence, and people with ADHD are not stupid, no. You can get to the level of the rest of your friends in class and even surpass that; it is the way you get there that can be different. Hyper focusing can also play an important role here because if you find something you enjoy doing, you will persevere until you get it right. Focusing on multiple things can also be an advantage because whilst others focus on one thing until they complete it and move to the next task, people with ADHD struggle to filter things, and this helps them put everything in perspective, seeing the bigger picture. Therefore people with ADHD are innovative and creative.

20. "Your handwriting is messy"- ADHD brains can race with ideas and can often jot down so many things randomly in their notebook. They know they can forget if they do not do so quickly. Some may struggle

with reading their handwriting, but they can go without you reminding them of this every time you cannot read what they have written.

21. "Are you even listening to me?"- People with ADHD have a hard time focusing, and the little distraction can take their minds into another different dimension. If you have a close friend or relative with ADHD, learn to adjust to their listening pace and ask them to stop you when they lose their focus on what you are saying. This will avoid embarrassment for them and frustrations for you.

22. "Can I borrow your meds?"- ADHDers on stimulant medication need to call their doctors monthly to get a new prescription every time. Navigating the healthcare system can be challenging for people with ADHD because they must have regular appointments, remember to call in for their medication on time, and remember to take them. If they fail to go by the system, they may need to pay hundreds out of their pocket or end up without medication for weeks. Abuse and misuse of stimulant medication have led to this complicated process that people who need this medication must go through every month. Dispensing is done accurately, and no medication can be bartered or exchanged, especially if it is a controlled drug like stimulant medication used for people with ADHD.

When you are unsure whether someone is truly lazy or has an underlying condition, rather than saying things that can come across as inconsiderate, try just being kind instead!

Chapter 28:
ADHD treatment for Women

A DHD is a condition that influences different parts of the mind, intellectual capacities, practices, and everyday life. Compelling treatment for ADHD in women may include a multimodal approach that incorporates medicine, psychotherapy, stress management, ADHD training as well as expert organizing techniques.

Indeed, even those women sufficiently lucky to get a precise ADHD analysis regularly face the resulting challenge of tracking down an expert who can give suitable treatment. Not many clinicians are experienced in treating grown-up ADHD, and surprisingly fewer know about the novel issues experienced by women with ADHD. Accordingly, most clinicians utilize standard psychotherapeutic methodologies. Albeit these methodologies can be useful in giving knowledge into enthusiastic and relational issues, they do not assist a woman with ADHD to figure out how to even more likely deal with her ADHD consistently or learn ways to lead a more gainful and fulfilling life. Medication does not build skills, and skills do not change the dopamine levels in the brain. So ADHD treatment should be planned by taking into consideration all available treatments to improve the overall life of a woman with ADHD.

ADHD-centered treatments are being created to address an expansive scope of issues, including confidence, relational and family issues, everyday wellbeing propensities, day-to-day anxiety, and life management abilities. Such medications are frequently alluded to as "neurocognitive psychotherapy," which joins intellectual conduct treatment with psychological recovery procedures. Intellectual conduct treatment centers around the mental issues of ADHD, for instance, confidence, self-acknowledgment, self-fault, while the psychological recovery approach centers around life management skills for improving psychological capacities like recollecting, understanding, critical thinking, assessing and utilizing judgment, learning compensatory methodologies, and rebuilding the environment.

Treatment for women with ADHD does not only include medication. The right treatment can be chosen with the help of your loved ones, taking into consideration your goals, and taking your doctor's advice.

Here are some treatment options for women with ADHD:

Medication- Prescription medication issues are frequently more muddled for women than for men. Any medicine approach needs to consider all parts of a woman's life, including the treatment of coinciding conditions which she might already be on. Women with ADHD are bound to experience the ill effects of coexisting disorders such as anxiety and depression, including learning incapacities. Since alcohol and substance abuse problems are common in women with ADHD and might be present at an early age, a cautious history of substance use needs to be taken into consideration when choosing the right treatment. Prescription medication might be additionally confounded by chemical variances across the hormonal changes and stages of life, for example, adolescence, perimenopause, and menopause, with an increment in ADHD side effects at whatever point estrogen levels fall. At times, chemical substitution may be incorporated into the treatment regime used to treat ADHD to make up for the lessened estrogen levels. ADHD medication helps to improve impulsivity and attention. ADHD treatment does not cure the condition but rather controls its symptoms when taken as prescribed. The same concept as prescription glasses, long or short-sightedness is not cured but rather controlled when wearing spectacles. Medication affects the transmission of molecules from one neuron to the next in the brain, mainly norepinephrine and dopamine. There can be a trial of medication at first, so physicians may determine what medication works best for each ADHD individual. Doses would be increased slowly until the desired benefits are achieved while also keeping an eye on any potential side effects.

Methylphenidate and amphetamines are two of the most common psychostimulant medication used for the management of ADHD. There are various brand names for these active ingredients, but because they are prone to abuse, they are highly controlled drugs. The user must see their doctor for monthly prescriptions and cannot be given refills without it. There are various preparations of these drugs; some that are long-acting and some short-acting. The long-acting ones would last anywhere from 6 to 12 hours for the newer preparations. Short-acting drugs would last approximately 4 hours. Long-acting medication may be preferred because people taking it would experience fewer mood fluctuations and can often stick to one fixed-dose daily rather than having to take multiple doses during the day, at work, or at school. Both long and short-acting drugs can be used together because some may feel the need for a booster in the afternoon and try to eliminate the rebound effect for when the long-acting drug does wear off, and the gap between this period and the next dosage the next day. Different drugs have different mechanisms of action, so the practitioner can base their assessment on this when choosing which drugs can work best for you. Depending on the individual sensitivity and severity of their ADHD, the long-acting drug might not be enough as a sole daily dose.

If an ADHD individual has a substance-use issue, this should be treated before treating ADHD. Stimulant medication is very well tolerated in therapeutic doses and if it is taken as prescribed and not abused. If an individual is prone to substance abuse and must take stimulant medication, the physician can opt for a drug that, because of its formulation and mechanism of action, is less likely to be abused. People who start taking stimulant medication can experience headaches, anxiety, weight loss, and some loss of appetite. Regular blood pressure monitoring is suggested for people with ADHD on stimulant medication, as cardiovascular effects have been reported but not deemed a risk for stroke or cardiac death. Stimulant medication is prescribed while taking into consideration the needs of the individual. Treatment is not set in stone and may change over time. A businesswoman with ADHD, who usually has meetings till late afternoon, might find an immediate-release drug to be taken in the afternoon beneficial when the sustained-release effect of the drug is wearing off. This can help her stay focused and carry on through her work schedule.

Non-stimulant medication is also a treatment option for people with ADHD who have an incomplete reaction to stimulant medication or have other psychiatric conditions. An example of non-stimulant medication for ADHD is Atomoxetine. This is not a controlled drug and can be prescribed over the phone with refills, unlike stimulant medication. Atomoxetine takes longer to act. People on this medication may experience cardiovascular side effects, decreased libido, loss of appetite, dry mouth, and insomnia. This drug is metabolized by the liver. Certain drugs like fluoxetine and paroxetine may inhibit the breakdown of atomoxetine, so it is very important to inform your physician of any other medication you might be on.

Antihypertensive treatment is rarely used in children and adults with ADHD but can be taken into consideration. These drugs affect norepinephrine levels to then affect dopamine levels. Antidepressants can directly increase neurotransmitters in the brain and can appear to improve ADHD symptoms. Antidepressant medication is not yet licensed to treat ADHD, depending on which regulatory board is considered for approval of medication in your area or country. However, such medication can still be considered as an off-license medication if your physicians believe this is the right treatment for you. Wake-promoting agents such as Modafinil are used to indirectly activate the frontal cortex without directly involving the central pathways for dopamine and norepinephrine in the brain. This is not the first line of treatment for people with ADHD, but when ADHDers on medication are not responsive to the most common treatments for ADHD, this can also be an option.

When choosing the right medication for your ADHD, your doctor will consider the negative effects of the drug, the characteristics of your ADHD, and your needs. If someone with ADHD also suffers from hypertension, not every drug is suitable for them, so an overall approach needs to be taken into consideration here. It is very important to monitor the effects of the medication, whether positive or negative.

Adjusting doses and timings for the medication can only be established by monitoring the effects of the drug. Try keeping track of your emotions during the day, when the drug has been taken, until its effects wear off. You may jot down notes in your journal or use a mobile app. During follow-up consultation, the doctor will ask for your feedback. This way, if you require additional treatment like therapy or coaching, this need can be met. The scope of ADHD medication is not only to treat the symptoms of ADHD, but the overall goal is to provide improved functioning in the real world. The goal of medication is to help ADHDers be self-sufficient and cope with the order of daily life. If taken as prescribed, ADHD medication can improve the functioning of a good quality lifestyle at the workplace, in school, and in interpersonal relationships.

If you have been diagnosed with ADHD and were previously diagnosed with another psychiatric disorder, it is important to decide which condition needs to be treated first according to its severity and its effects on your daily life. For example, if someone has been long diagnosed with depression and has now been diagnosed with ADHD, certain medication can exacerbate depressive symptoms. Selective serotonin reuptake inhibitors, also known as SSRIs, are used in depression and can be used with stimulant medication for ADHD in harmony. If ADHD was the undiagnosed condition, treating this as the main issue can help treat the other co-existing conditions. If ADHD is the main concern, treating it first can improve the other symptoms.

Stimulant medication is the first line of treatment for ADHD, although this is surrounded by a stigma, and ADHDers often make decisions about treatments based on the stigma around medicating ADHD.

Stimulant medication for ADHD can often be considered on the same line as illegal drugs like cocaine, when for the individual with ADHD, that medication is giving them a second chance at life, without having to worry of not fitting in or never making the cut. Stimulant medication cannot be generalized as any other drug and if taken with caution and as prescribed. People with untreated ADHD are at a higher risk of drug and alcohol dependence and not the other way round. People with undiagnosed or misdiagnosed ADHD tend to use illegal drugs to compensate for their ADHD symptoms, depression, or anxiety, which has been left untreated. Taking medication for your ADHD is not succumbing to the condition you have because there is nothing wrong with taking medication that will help correct the neurotransmitter deficit in your brain, just as if you have anemia and take iron supplements to treat it.

Parent training- Women with ADHD are more likely to have a child with ADHD. A lot of women understand they have ADHD when one of their kids is diagnosed. They realize that whatever their child is going through right now, they experienced during their childhood. Parenting requires the mother to be the manager of the house and juggle multiple duties like cleaning, setting appointments, and cooking. This requires a lot of focus, organization, and planning. These are all areas women with ADHD struggle with. Parenting tools can help women in managing their household duties, kids' upbringing, and the pressure at work on top of everything. Parent training can be done in groups or individually. Some may attend group classes where basic skills are thought to help women with ADHD cope with their lives as mothers.

Group therapy- Women with ADHD can struggle with their self-esteem and social interactions. They often compare themselves with other women and feel shame. Group therapy can provide women with ADHD with a therapeutic experience and help them feel accepted and understood. This can help them accept themselves and better manage their lives. During group therapy, partners of women with ADHD may be invited to share their experiences and how they deal with their partner's ADHD. Hearing people sharing similar experiences to yours can nest hope in that woman with ADHD that often felt out of place in the world. Women with ADHD may compare themselves to neurotypical brains and decide to strive for perfection when this is often unrealistic. Therapy can help eliminate these guilt factors and improve overall confidence and self-esteem in women with ADHD.

ADHD coaching- ADHD coaches will help you via the phone, via email, or in person. ADHD coaching is a newer sector that has gained popularity in recent years. Coaching is a non-pharmacologic technique that can be used in conjunction with treatment. ADHD coaching is a practical technique that directly addresses the core impairments of ADHD, such as preparation, time management, goal setting, organization, and motivation. It is a specialization within the wider area of coaching. ADHD mentors work cooperatively with their clients with ADHD or ADHD-like manifestations to address their specific necessities and individual objectives. Most current ADHD instructing programs recognize the natural underpinnings of the problem affecting the main manifestations of ADHD like absentmindedness, hyperactivity, and impulsivity. Nonetheless, training focuses on the scholastic, professional, passionate, and relational life troubles that are a consequence of these side effects and assists customers with discovering approaches to conquer these difficulties. Through individualized or group help and backing, mentors help individuals focus on where they are currently, where they need to be and how they get there. A mentor assists individuals with ADHD complete the down-to-earth exercises of everyday life in a coordinated, objective-oriented, and opportune manner. In close association, an ADHD mentor assists the ADHDer with mastering viable abilities and start a change in their day-to-day life. Women with ADHD can be aided by a coach to maintain focus, come up with goals, achieve set goals, bring their abstract ideas to fruition, and build motivation. An ADHD coach will also help sufferers to identify what their symptoms of ADHD are and how they play an important role in their lives. They can help them identify their behaviors in certain situations and which ones are attributed to their ADHD. An ADHD coach may ask the sufferer what changes they want in their lives, what steps can be taken to get to those goals, what motivates them to take action, what actions they've taken toward their goals, and when they want to achieve set goals. The coach will ask about steps already taken and what is left to be done, if any. Evaluation needs to be done. Coaches are there to help support their clients through feedback and practical suggestions. Another thing coaches do is hold you accountable. ADHDers can struggle to complete tasks if they are not held accountable. They can be there to help remind you and suggest better management methods you can adapt. Coaches have an initial session to identify the goals they wish to achieve by providing their services to the client, but regular check-ins and follow-up sessions are carried out. These can be done virtually or in person. Initial sessions can take up to 2 hours and may not be enough to go over all the issues one intends to address, but follow-up sessions can take up to 60 minutes each time. During the sessions, reflection is made whilst discussing whether last week's goals were met, how and what can be improved, and what is the goal for the next session. Once goals are met after several sessions, the ADHD sufferer may choose to extend the coaching sessions or terminate the service. During this period, the ADHDer would have obtained skills and learned how to adapt them. The goal is to carry on putting these skills into practice without the constant need of a coach. Studies show that coaching improves executive functioning skills and determination skills in college kids. People under the care of a coach can develop more positive thoughts and manners. They can take up greater responsibilities, where before, these were avoided. They can better regulate their stress levels and emotions, where before, emotional dysregulation was often present. Coached women with ADHD can improve their studying and learning skills and report to be more self-aware and satisfied in life overall. Coaching can be done on an individual basis or as a group. Coaching is targeted as a wellness model, and dealing with psychological barriers is usually left in the hands of a therapist. It is more focused on daily living like practical habits in everyday life, lifestyle changes, managing finances, and maintaining a healthy nutrition and exercise regime. Cognitive-behavioral therapy deals with the emotional side of things, so these two fields do not overlap. Coaches would not be trained to deal with psychiatric issues and can only focus on practical changes. A psychotherapist or psychologist will deal with the emotional aspect and cannot help with regards to practical aspects of life like the coach would. The "why" of an ADHD behavior is better dealt with by a therapist. Coaching is different than tutoring. Tutoring is more common in kids who struggle in certain subjects in school and would rather have some extra hours on the subject via one-to-one encounters to keep up with the class curriculum. Before choosing coaching as a non-pharmacological intervention for your ADHD, you must accept that there is an issue and decide to want to make changes. Coaching can require time to create strategies and improve your behavior, so willingness is a must. If an ADHD coach feels like his intervention is not yielding its benefits, he or she may refer you if the need for a psychiatric assistant is required. Referrals do not mean coaching will seize, but rather the ADHD coach can work in collaboration with a therapist or a psychiatrist to help improve your overall state of ADHD. There are plenty of services as such, and one must consider their own situation and question whether they require a coach specializing in any area. If you feel like any specific approach can work best for you; like humorous or energetic, and if you struggle with comorbid conditions like anxiety or depression, make sure coaching is the right type of treatment for you, or if it is best to combine it with other alternative therapy treatments to get the best results.

Behavioral therapy- Cognitive behavioral therapy is also known as CBT and is often used in conjunction with medication. There are various types of therapy, and CBT is one of them. CBT works on how your thoughts affect your emotions and behavior. CBT also provides you with tools to help manage these thoughts. Another type of therapy is dialectic behavioral therapy, also known as DBT. This can help with emotional dysregulation, a common effect of ADHD. It can also help with mindfulness and increase your ability to notice your thoughts and feelings and not react to them. This treatment is provided by either a psychologist or a psychotherapist. A therapist can help you by providing you with a different perspective and solutions outside your brain, but at the same time, resolutions that are tailored to you. A therapist takes into consideration what you know about ADHD, what you have tried to do to control it so far, what works for you, and where your current tools can be used. They can help you change the way you use your tools or help you develop new ones. It is common to get different diagnoses from different therapists because ADHD shares symptoms with other conditions like depressions and anxiety. Most people with ADHD can suffer from one or more of the other conditions, and the latter can be more recognizable than the formal. Not every therapist will understand ADHD, and some may also claim to specialize in ADHD because of their clinical work, research studies, or experience working with ADHD clients. Various tests can be used to evaluate ADHD, and the therapist can use whatever source is available to them. ADHD is determined depending on the number of symptoms and level of impairment, and this is all subjective. The therapist will focus on alleviating ADH-related impairments while a psychiatrist can help you reduce the symptoms with the help of medication. Ideally, following therapy sessions, you leave feeling optimistic and look forward to the next session. You must feel comfortable enough with your therapist so you can discuss your issues, and he or she can help you grow. Initially, you can start with the first session with the therapist, often referred to as Intake, where the therapist would gather information about your ADHD and the goals you wish to achieve. It is important that you feel heard and validated during therapy. You must feel comfortable enough to ask whatever questions you like. Building a good therapeutic relationship during the third or fourth session can usually mean you are more likely to gain success out of this treatment. Progress can fluctuate because this can be affected by various life events. Your therapist will keep a record of your progress, so check in with them whenever possible because they might notice the progress you have made from time to time, but you have not realized it.

Professional Organizing- The organizer career has expanded to meet the demand as modern lives have become more complicated. Women with ADHD often experience extreme disorganization in a variety of areas of their lives, in their house, and at work. Some women can keep their workplaces organized but at the cost of their homes being a complete mess. Some ADHDers may compensate by becoming overly organized, but this is rarely the case in women with ADHD. Disorganization is common among other areas of a woman's life, which adds to the problems and difficulties. You may hire someone who can do the organizing for you if you lack the skill in this sector; otherwise, you may conduct sessions with a professional organizer who can help you get organized in your daily life, after which you will be able to maintain a relatively organized lifestyle after the sessions are over.

Career Guidance- Women with ADHD can benefit greatly from career guidance, which can help them take advantage of their strengths while minimizing the effect of ADHD on job success, much as they may benefit greatly from clear guidance as a parent with ADHD. Many technical and office occupations require a person with ADHD to perform tasks and duties that are difficult for them, such as paying attention to detail. Some companies may impose certain ways or methods to be used to reach set targets. These methods might not always work for women with ADHD. This is not to say that they cannot reach set targets, but their methods are different than neurotypical brains. There are careers and job posts that will allow their employees the flexibility they need if results are promising. Not every career allows this, so career guidance can help a woman with ADHD choose the right path for her and highlight her strengths rather than putting her down for her weaknesses.

Medication-assisted treatment for ADHD is particularly effective at reducing the main symptoms of the disorder like inattention, hyperactivity, and impulsivity. Your healthcare provider will assist you in selecting the appropriate drug and dosage for your specific requirements. It's important to work with your doctor to track your care and manage any side effects you may have. The most effective treatment for ADHD is to combine medicine with therapeutic treatments such as parent education training and behavioral therapy. There are various aspects of life where women with ADHD will struggle, but thankfully there are various approaches that provide either general help for these issues or specific assistance according to the weakness one may experience exclusively. ADHD is deserving of treatment like any other medical condition.

Chapter 29:
Self-love for women with ADHD

T he ADHD brain can go into extreme mentality. The issue is that humans are complex and inconsistent. Consequently, often women with ADHD oscillate between intense views of themselves; poor or nice, stupid or clever, driven or lazy. This reactive, intense thought contributes to low self-esteem, which can be supplemented by inward thought and a good dose of self-compassion. You probably grew up believing that you were either smart or stupid, happy or unhappy, sweet or rude. Maybe you feel good and optimistic one day, then the next you were exhausted, even frozen, by your ADHD symptoms and depressive thoughts. You can still be experiencing these feelings to date. Changing views and mood swings are not exclusive to the ADHD brain. Everyone goes through cycles of delusional thoughts and periods of clarity. One may feel guilty when screaming at someone they care about, but then be nice to strangers. Everyone is different at all moments, often within the same day. This is natural, but these human contradictions are disturbing and confounding to the ADHD brain. The ADHD brain thinks in terms of extreme polarities: inspired vs. lazy, imaginative vs. dull, ordered vs. disorganized. Your subconscious is compelled to take sides. However, when humans are always evolving and vacillating, this neurological phenomenon leaves them flip-flopping from day to day, reduced to reactivity rather than deliberate thinking and behavior.

Kids with ADHD grew up being told they did something wrong more than neurotypical kids every day. It is estimated that kids with ADHD are given five times more corrective messages than neurotypical brains every day. This can go on into adulthood if you are a woman with undiagnosed or misdiagnosed ADHD. Eventually, this negative talk will become your inner dialogue, and you start believing the negative feedback you are being given or have been given for most of your life. It can be hard to get oneself out of this deeply ingrained negative self-thought. Although it can be challenging, you can talk yourself out of this negativity and enhance trust in yourself despite whatever you have been told as a kid or growing up. Once you receive negative feedback, acknowledge it but do not let it get to you. Acknowledge and understand you have a condition, and your behavior is a result of your symptoms. This is not making up excuses but acknowledging the fact that the reason you missed out on an important conversation from that meeting you just had, and are now being scolded for, did not happen on purpose and not because you are careless. It is because of your ADHD. Much like someone who needs prescription glasses who has run over a stray cat on their way home from work late at night. It is not because they meant to do that, but because of their impaired vision, they could hardly have avoided that incident. Acknowledging your ADHD can make room for you to grow. If you know you are chronically late, you can try and do better next time. Beating yourself up and thinking you are a horrible person will not get you anywhere besides filling you with negative thoughts and emotions. Try engaging in positive self-talk to help to get you past your negative self-talk. If you are surrounded by the right people and happen to feel down because of something you did or failed to do because of your ADHD, try calling someone you know and trust. Explain what happened and ask them to help you talk yourself out of the negative self-talk. Make sure you are well educated about your

ADHD. Understanding your condition, its symptoms, and how it may exhibit in different people can help you understand and validate your actions. ADHD awareness can help you understand yourself and empower you to know how to deal with yourself and daily challenges. To heal, you must be able to keep all of who you are in one picture that encompasses a wide range of characteristics. That means no longer dwelling only on your problems or your strengths. You partake in reductionism as you overemphasize one part of oneself and ignore the others. You oversimplify or exaggerate one aspect of yourself. Moving into a more complete narrative necessitates a break from reductionism and the completion of the whole image of oneself. Women with ADHD have been given so much shame in their lives that they think they cannot live with their ADHD unless they correct themselves. Certainly, ADHD influences who you are, and coping with your brain-based problems is unavoidable. Accept that you cannot completely differentiate your minds and bodies is a positive development. You must allow yourself to think you can do a task or complete a project, even though it might be a struggle to do so. This can take you away from the two extremities, one of which is often thinking you will fail or are better off not even trying. This can make room for self-improvement and positive thinking. When you come to know you have a condition, you often want to find the fix for it. The reality is that there is no permanent fix that can have you fit in and perform like neurotypical brains but focusing on improvement and self-awareness can help you complete tasks via different methods. It is normal to struggle with this concept and to have moments where you wish your ADHD would all go away. True recovery, on the other hand, comes only through the act of convincing yourself and others that you do not need to be fixed. Once you agree that it is understandable and natural to have both strengths and weaknesses, you begin to address the struggles with some self-compassion, and this is the secret to seeing positive progress. You are well-versed in the difficulties associated with ADHD. In fairness, you have been overly dependent on them your whole life. Drawing an accurate portrait of yourself entails giving equal weight to your talents and dreams that represent your ideals. However, many people are unaware of these places or find them difficult to navigate. To help navigate your ADHD, start by becoming aware of your strengths and take note of what you do well. Acknowledge the fact that you have acquired skills and developed through the years. Be aware of your challenges and your weaknesses and how this affects you in your daily life. Leave room for these weaknesses even if you are on ADHD medication, as your ADHD symptoms might not always be fully under control. Try thinking about how you react in certain situations and how your ADHD is exhibited in different walks of life. Endorse the good qualities you have in life and how you adapt these in different situations. People speak a lot about the relevance of ideas, but they rarely use them as a guideline. To know what humans want their lives to be like, women who are controlled by the push and pull of the ADHD brain must look inward and return to an internal compass. When you feel like you are running around in circles, take a moment to tell yourself who you are and what is important to you. When you feel confused or mentally exhausted, following your internal compass, your beliefs, rather than the distractions of ADHD, will direct smarter decisions. If you have determined what you admire, you should create a personal mission statement in the same way you would if you were running your own company. After all, you are in control of your destiny.

Start living by your values and define what is meaningful to you. Become aware of what you want your life to be about and what you represent. Identify your values and what you want people to come to know about you. Take into consideration your past experiences, what you made of them and what you have to say about yourself.

Self-esteem refers to how you see yourself. It is your assessment of your abilities and weaknesses. People with high self-esteem can admire their talents while still being sympathetic about their shortcomings. They esteem themselves and expect people to honor them. This means that they do not settle for less than they deserve. They do not beat themselves up for failing or not trying hard enough. They do not accept being part of an abusive relationship because they are not deserving of love. People with ADHD have numerous traumatic memories and life events because of ADHD symptoms such as poor focus, forgetfulness, and the desire for instant gratification. For example, they may struggle with academic underachievement, career issues, or social issues such as making and maintaining friends and interpersonal relationships. These disappointing experiences and shortcomings harm their self-esteem. Bad experiences and mistakes harm your self-esteem. As a result, you begin to question your skills and talents. To end the loop and begin improving your self-esteem, you must first believe in yourself. Believing in yourself can sound boring and predictable, but trusting your strengths and skills is a wonderful first step toward raising your self-esteem. According to research, individuals with ADHD may be extremely adaptive and will be able to adjust continuously, but improvement is inevitable regardless of the background. This is called resilience, the ability to recover from failed targets and try again. This means not giving up and using your failures to succeed.

Women with ADHD may struggle with this personality trait because they have been told they cannot do it numerous times. They were given duties in society as women or mothers, and because they often struggle to complete these tasks or fit in society, they may have been told to quit or give up more times than they can remember. Resilience is striving to be better and ignoring the negative energy around you telling you to give up. Women with ADHD may struggle to be resilient because of how they have been taught to perceive themselves. With the help of professionals and the right circle around you, you can learn how to become resilient. Go to people you trust and know can understand you when you feel like giving up. If you cannot remind yourself of the strengths and good qualities you hold, those around you can. So, when you feel discouraged, do reach out to someone you know can help you get out of despair. Remind yourself that someone or many people around you believe in you and can help keep you on track.

Contrary to all the negative comments you received as a kid, use that energy to fuel your resilience and prove them wrong. If you feel that your efforts do not matter, try volunteering. It can make you feel so accomplished and helpful. Do not focus your energy on negative feedback only. Try to recall positive feedback you received in the past and use it to empower yourself to try again. It does not have to be feedback related to that struggle you are facing; use whatever you can to help boost your self-esteem. Enable no one to make you doubt yourself. If they criticize something you did, cut yourself some slack and consider some of the things you have done right, and remind yourself that not everything you do is a complete disaster.

People are all born with their own set of skills and abilities. If you are not sure, spend the next week observing which tasks and behaviors come naturally to you. Which ones do you love performing, and on which do you get compliments? All of those are hints! Take note of the things people ask you for help or come to you for opinions on; that is a clear example of your strengths. Spending time remembering these details is a quick way to boost your self-esteem. Rather than attempting to improve at jobs that are difficult for you, devote the rest of your effort to activities at which you excel. Apply this principle to all aspects of your life, including employment, home, hobbies, and so on. This does not mean you refuse to work on anything you do not do well, your weaknesses, or the skills you lack most. Besides relying on your strengths, there are some fundamental qualities you must master to excel in life and feel good about yourself. Because of the way your ADHD brain functions, these abilities may not come easily to you. However, with practice, they are possible to master. Keep in mind that improving your skills can benefit you. Arriving on time to appointments or meetings can make you feel reliable. Managing your money well can help you avoid overspending and forgetting due bills, can, in turn, boost your self-esteem because you do not feel like you are being eaten away by your debt. If you master the skill of meal planning and healthy eating, it can, in turn, make you feel your best because you are no longer surviving on junk food and unhealthy meals. If you learn how to manage your house, you can no longer be crippled by a dirty house full of clutter and can finally enjoy time with family and friends when they come over to visit, instead of feeling embarrassed. These activities could be more difficult for you because they require abilities that ADHD makes challenging. It is, however, possible to excel at any of them. How you were rewarded and punished as a kid has an impact on how you see yourself now and then. Children with ADHD are more likely to earn disapproval than encouragement.

As an adult, you may dwell on anything you did bad or poorly because it has become your default mode. From now on, for any critique you direct at yourself, consider two positive aspects of yourself. This can help to rebalance things and boost your self-esteem. You may have developed the habit of comparing yourself to others as a teenager. Unwillingly you may have been compared to others all the time, in class or within your family. Your siblings, relatives, and peers can most likely do stuff you find difficult, such as pay attention in class or stay still. When you compare yourself negatively to others, it undermines your self-esteem.

You are too hard on yourself, which induces actual physical and emotional discomfort. Rather than focusing on your supposed failures, consider these uplifting ways to recognize your worth. Adults with ADHD are good at putting themselves down and being much harsher on themselves. They are more tolerant and accepting of their mates' blunders than they are of their own. Self-criticism is a behavior that many people develop as children. A child with ADHD notices his parents' and teachers' dissatisfaction with him, and he does not feel well enough. The kid spends his early years striving to impress others and, as a result, starts to judge himself harshly. By the teen years, some children are always working desperately for recognition from teachers and guardians, while others have given up and believe they are still losers.

I have a strategy for you if you tend to focus on your flaws. Everyone has flaws, and no one is flawless. Things you have done should not lower your self-esteem or make the impression that you are not good enough. You are sufficient, whether you have accomplished something or not. You may have spent far too much time dwelling on your flaws and weaknesses that you have forgotten about your talents. Make a list of your innate strengths, gifts, and expertise. This could include your easy-going personality towards others, your sense of humor or narrative style, your sincerity, or your willingness to work well with others. You will learn and develop your skills. Do not abandon something you like just because you are not good at it right now. Get the training or practice you need to transform your threats into opportunities. It is difficult enough to have ADHD without dealing with family and friends who criticize you for your struggles. Seek people who admire and value your qualities. Begin by doing an impartial appraisal of those whose comments are harmful and damaging, and then either teach them about ADHD or limit your interaction with them. If your mother still hopes you are more like your sister or if your brother demoralizes you when he calls, then stops answering their phone calls! You are not allowed to detach from your family, but you may restrict the amount of time you spend with them. Being in the company of people who admire you will cause you to think more positively of yourself, paving the path to satisfaction and prosperity. Measure yourself against your expectations. True self-esteem is unaffected by the views of others. To do this, you will need to consult with a mental health specialist to rewrite the scripts that have been playing in your mind for a long time if this is something you still find yourself struggling with despite all efforts.

Stop describing yourself based on your ADHD symptoms. You may have ADHD, but it does not own you. A condition is just one aspect of who you are. Learn to appreciate the other aspects of yourself and allow yourself to feel strong enough to acknowledge some level of self-worth!

Chapter 30:
How mindfulness practice can benefit Women with ADHD

W omen who have ADHD face stressful events and pressures. Meditation, with or without ADHD drugs, should be part of the management regimen that increases the quality of life. According to research, meditation may help reduce destructive ADHD-related symptoms, including difficulty concentrating and impulsivity.

Women with ADHD have traditionally been an underserved category and pay a high price as a result. A delayed diagnosis, a misdiagnosis, and a lack of real ADHD knowledge translate to years of unnecessary struggle, poor self-esteem, being marginalized, and thinking something is flawed with them. As a result, women with ADHD can benefit greatly from mindfulness, which is an excellent tool for improving health and reducing the burden of living with an often misunderstood disorder. Some women can go their entire life without ever realizing they have ADHD. This can be a very upsetting feeling for many women, who all too frequently find themselves in the unfortunate situation of "moving on" without assistance when an adequate diagnosis could greatly change their lives. Furthermore, those who seek treatment with possible signs run the risk of being misdiagnosed with another illness, such as mood disturbance or anxiety. The result, though, remains the same: a lack of assistance and care for the appropriate conditions, which could contribute to more mental health issues. Women with ADHD often experience profound tension as they try to maintain an outwardly natural character that satisfies social demands and desires while simultaneously coping with an influx of ADHD symptoms frequently compounded by changing hormones over time. This dynamic can also contribute to burnouts daily. Females with ADHD sometimes conceal how much time it takes to get through each day, secretly wondering how other women seem to have it so simple. Meanwhile, their stray thoughts, interests, and sacrifices are overlooked in a society that struggles to accommodate minds that think differently. It is not shocking that living this way can lead to increased anxiety, feelings of inferiority, and deterioration of self-esteem over time. It is difficult to be accused of being dreamy or careless when you are trying nonstop to keep life going, feeling bad when it fails, and drained when it is complete. Overall, the feeling can be debilitating, leaving those who are masking ADHD in desperate need of help.

Meditation may not be the only means of treating your ADHD, but it can help to ease the symptoms. There are many forms of meditation, which means that there is one that works better on your brain. Personalized mantras, for example, can be especially powerful due to their familiarity. Mantra meditation, as opposed to deliberately focusing on silencing a busy or disturbed mind, asks you to repeat a sentence in your head and let it take you naturally to a place of peace and rest. So, consider the right methods of meditations if you are a woman with ADHD because not all forms work. Mantra meditation has the virtue of providing little space for the mind to drift. This is one of the most difficult obstacles for beginners of meditations and women with ADHD and those who suffer the most with concentration. This refocusing of the mind, if performed daily, will help clear your mind and strengthen your concentration.

Meditation, in addition to its relaxing and de-stressing properties, can help develop communication abilities over time by promoting pauses and contemplation. Women with better communication skills are less likely to be stressed in meetings and social settings and can strike a happy medium while communicating with others. This can help women with ADHD control their impulsivity, letting them have better communication in their daily lives, which in turn will alleviate stress during usually uncomfortable situations.

Meditation allows your brain and body to reach a deeper resting state than even your longest sleep. Tapping into this state allows the prefrontal cortex to fully relax. As a result, cortisol and other stress chemicals are decreased by up to a quarter, while happy hormone output increases, leaving you even more resistant to unwanted yet unavoidable future stress. This is vital for women with ADHD because it alleviates stress and paranoia while also building morale and encouraging them to be more loyal to themselves. Meditation can be performed whenever and wherever the individual requires it, making it the ideal, independent method for ADHD symptom control. Although meditation is not a substitute for ADHD treatment, it can be used as part of a holistic recovery strategy to greatly contribute to the betterment of women with ADHD. Mindfulness and meditation enable you to devote attention to your emotions and emotional wellbeing so that you do not behave recklessly and respond differently to tense situations.

After a lifetime of rushing emotions, it can be difficult to picture yourself happily seated in the lotus pose. You do not have to sit or even quit moving to meditate, which is a little-known secret. You can meditate using music. It does not need to be in silence. You can use melody to practice your breathing patterns. It is acceptable to have your thoughts drift away from meditation. Try to disengage and move your focus back to meditation. You can find yourself doing this multiple times at first, and that is fine. Understand that meditation is something that requires practice, and there is no right or wrong in this. Do this activity not to judge yourself but to better your state of mind. When you meditate, calm your agitated body with quick, repeated motions such as walking. Start by meditating for a few minutes a day and increase the time as it becomes more manageable. Try to stick to it and make this a habit. If you find it hard to stick to this as a routine, try enrolling in a meditation course or organize regular meet-ups with a close friend. You can make use of mobile applications as well. Meditation can help you deal with difficult feelings at work or home. It helps you to take a step back from the chaos and concentrate on your relevant field. You can keep seeing both optimistic and bad interactions. However, if you learn to relax and control your tension, you and those around you can enjoy the happiness you deserve. Throw out your preconceived notions of meditation because you do not have to sit silently to do it. Most meditation applications are online. Download a lot, then pick your favorite. Perhaps a certain narrator's voice irritates you, or another's tone appeals to you more than the others. Each application begins with a step-by-step explanation of how to be conscious. Breathing seems to be easy, doesn't it? Breathing is the first ability you must learn before you can meditate to control your concentration and feelings, which might sound strange. You start by counting to five as you breathe in and counting to seven as you breathe out. There is no magic number; just take as many breaths as you feel comfortable. It is difficult to plan your time while you have ADHD. Finding time for yourself is much more difficult. Some hardly have time to take a shower, let alone meditate for a half-hour a day. When you first start to meditate, you can notice that your response to physical stress changes. You no longer get a feeling of overwhelm, and if you do, it can be much easier to get rid of that feeling. Prioritizing can get easier with the help of meditation too. It can feel easier to decide which tasks need to be tackled first. Once you master meditation, you should be able to function better at home and work. You should stop striving to be perfect and believe you are the best version of yourself. Meditation can help you hinder your negative self-talk and change the way you think and look at yourself. According to research, cognitive meditation for ADHD will teach the brain to properly concentrate and maintain focus. Keeping focus and managing to self-regulate are two persistent regular obstacles for both adults and children with ADHD. As a normal ADHD treatment, it stands to reason that any kind of concentration training that also improves self-control will be invaluable and extremely effective.

Mindful meditation, also known as mindfulness, is used in various religious cultures. Buddhism, for example, includes a form of mindful practice known as vipassana. If you are not spiritual or religious, it does not mean you cannot meditate. It entails paying careful attention to your emotions, feelings, and physiological sensations; in other words, having a better sense of what is going on with you at any given time. It can be used to promote health, especially psychological well-being. Similar methods have been used to treat chronic pain, fatigue, and mood disturbances, as well as to reduce blood pressure. ADHD medication cannot work on inner skills, unlike meditation. It helps to increase your capacity to self-observe, train attention, and build new relationships to stressful experiences, strengthening your ability to monitor your attention. In other words, it helps you to give heed to paying attention, and it will also make people more mindful of their psychological response, preventing them from reacting recklessly. For a long time, researchers have discussed using meditation to treat ADHD, but the challenge has always been whether people with ADHD can use it, particularly if they are overactive. Mindfulness's adaptability and simplicity allow for individuality in the strategy, allowing it to fit for you. The trick is to practice mindfulness during your day, constantly being conscious of where your concentration is directed when doing repetitive tasks. For instance, you might find that your mind wanders when driving. Many people exercise mindfulness as they snack. Once you are used to tuning in with yourself and your body, you can use the practice whenever you're feeling stressed.

Meditation can be something you master on your own if you know you can stick to this new commitment together with your already busy routine. Sit in a quiet spot where you cannot be interrupted for five minutes, concentrating on the feeling of breathing in and out, paying attention to how your stomach peaks and drops. You might soon find that you are worried about something else; your career, a noise you just overhead, or your plans for later in the day. Mark these ideas as "thought," and then refocus your attention on meditating and breathing. Do this mental exercise regularly. Increase the amount of time you spend on the workout every couple of days if you notice you can. Do this during the day, reflecting on your breath for a few minutes as you stroll from place to place, at a traffic light, or while seated at your workstation. You may exercise mindfulness at any moment, even when conversing with others. Turning on the mind-awareness state at any point during the day, even for a few minutes, is an excellent practice. It is simply letting go of the hustle of the mind and focusing on what is happening in the current moment of the daily situation.

Distraction is in the essence of the subconscious. Mindful consciousness is about returning to the breath rather than sticking in it. That is what improves your ability to concentrate. You do not need help breathing because that is already an involuntary action of the body. You use breathing to help control your thoughts and re-center your mind. It is the focus on re-shifting your concentration, on outwitting the mind's normal propensity to escape, that makes this approach particularly useful for anyone with ADHD.

In contrast to other therapies, mindfulness therapy does not require a prescription or a visit to a clinic. You can do it while seated, walking, or even doing certain kinds of yoga. When a muscle is fragile, you can strengthen it with workouts. The same goes for your brain. Meditation is believed to help with ADHD since it thickens the prefrontal cortex, which is involved with concentration, planning, and impulse regulation. It also increases the amount of dopamine in the brain, which is in low supply in ADHD brains. Yoga has also been found to help relieve ADHD symptoms, though most of the studies have been conducted on adolescents. It increases dopamine levels and activates the prefrontal cortex, much like mindful practice. According to research, people with ADHD can meditate effectively, and meditation can help some of the habits associated with the condition.

Some people feel that meditating first thing early in the morning helps them cope with the stresses of the day. Early morning meditation can also help you incorporate it into your routine before your daily routines begin, and you are less likely to put it off to later during the day because things seem more important. If you are a night owl or have trouble falling asleep, meditating before bedtime might be a safer option for you. There is never a bad time to meditate. Find whatever works for you. No one posture is more conducive to meditation than another. Traditional poses are appealing to some individuals. However, you can meditate either seated in your comfortable chair or lying down on the couch. Whatever location you choose, make sure it is comfortable enough for you to hold for the length of your meditation session.

Make sure the location you chose is quiet with no to minimal distractions. It can be more difficult to calm your mind if your trousers are uncomfortable or your sweater itches. The same is true for earrings or shoes that are too tight. Wear clothes that fit well and are comfortable for you. Place yourself in a calm, distraction-free environment, free of mobile device reminders such as text messaging and incoming emails. Close the door or go into a room where you can be quiet for the duration of your meditation if possible. It is possible to meditate effectively even though you live in a city or on a busy street. Meditation, through repetition, will teach you to ignore distractions by concentrating on your breathing techniques. You can also block out sounds by meditating to soft music or using a guided meditation program if you prefer. Meditation incorporates the internal experience of breathing to get the consciousness back to the current moment. Begin by naturally breathing in and out, noticing how it makes the body feel. When you are ready, take a deep breath in and notice how your body feels. Hold your breath for a few seconds, then exhale softly for as long as your breath allows. Take note of how the body responds when it exhales. When your mind wanders away from the present moment, quickly remember the sensation, and return your attention to your breathing. Accept that thinking is the essence of the mind and grant yourself consent to have a wandering mind. Do not criticize yourself or concentrate your mind on your emotions. Simply return your consciousness to the present moment by concentrating on your breathing. If you meditate for one minute or thirty, allow yourself a few seconds or minutes to return to the current moment after the experience. Open your eyes if they were closed. Take a minute to observe what is going on around you. Take note of how the body feels. Take a minute to recognize your feelings and ideas. Much like you allow time for yourself to get out of bed in the morning, allow time for yourself to get out of your mindful state.

Meditation is not easy, and it will not heal ADHD. It can be a challenge to master meditation when you have ADHD. But it can help you train your mind to work better under higher levels of stress and more demanding situations. Allow your mind to explore and decide what works better for you during meditation. More research on the efficacy of mindfulness on symptoms of ADHD is required, but the research on this natural ADHD treatment is positive so far.

Chapter 31:
ADHD myths and facts

T hose who have not come across or know someone close to them who suffers from ADHD may still struggle to understand and believe ADHD is real. There are so many misconceptions that create confusion and make it difficult for people with ADHD to get the help they need at school, work, and in society in general. The evidence from scientific findings continues to debunk ADHD stereotypes and misconceptions.

Here are some ADHD myths and facts to help overcome some misconceptions: -

#1-ADHD is not a real disorder.

A lot of people think ADHD is not like any other medical condition. A lot of research has been done over time confirming ADHD is very much real, and although the name of this condition has been changed from time to time, it was confirmed by multiple studies that ADHD exists. The name ADHD was made up by researchers to describe this condition and has replaced previous outdated names like minimal brain damage, as used in the past. ADHD is one of the most researched mental health conditions. It has been established that ADHD is a neurodevelopmental disorder. A lot of health centers and psychiatric associations recognize ADHD as a real disorder. Brain imaging is being used to prove differences in the brain of people with ADHD. Needless to say, those who have ADHD do more than recognize ADHD as a real condition but also live with it.

#2-ADHD is a fancy name for bad behavior.

To those who do not know much about ADHD, it may come across as laziness or bad behavior. What most overlook and fail to consider is that behavior is controlled by the brain. ADHD is affected by genetics, and they leave their effects on the brain. Those with ADHD are often trying very hard to pay attention and sit still. Thinking people with ADHD can just focus is like asking someone who suffers from short-sightedness to see better. Neurodiverse brains do not battle with attention because of an attitude but because of the differences in their brain function when compared to neurotypical brains.

#3-ADHD is just for kids.

Kids diagnosed with ADHD cannot grow out of ADHD. Some adults may still experience ADHD symptoms, but these will not affect them to the point where their lives are impaired. That does not mean that they have outgrown ADHD. A huge portion of people with ADHD are not diagnosed until they became adults. Some adults may be diagnosed when one of their kids is diagnosed because ADHD is hereditary, and if your kid has it, it is very likely one of the parents does too. Kids with ADHD grow up to become adults with ADHD. They learn to cope with their symptoms and find ways to overcome their difficulties, but that does not mean they have outgrown this disorder.

#4-ADHD is caused by bad parenting, sugar consumption, or excessive gaming.

ADHD is influenced by changes in the brain, not by poor parenting. Some adults, though, see children fidgeting, acting impulsively, or not concentrating and conclude it is due to a lack of control. They are unaware that what they are seeing are symptoms of a serious disorder rather than the product of something their parents or guardians did or did not do. Although some of these factors can worsen symptoms of ADHD, these of themselves do not cause ADHD. High sugar intake can cause hyperactivity or exacerbate ADHD symptoms, but it does not cause the condition in the first place. If parents are overly critical of their kids, it can have adverse reactions on kids with ADHD, but it does not mean that criticizing your child can cause him to suffer from ADHD. Kids with ADHD need all the support they can get and require their parents, as their support system, to help them get through the challenges. These challenges can be very hard to handle if you are an adult, let alone a kid who is completely dependent on an adult for medication, therapy, other forms of treatment, and organizational aid. Research shows that rather than blaming an ADHD diagnosis on their bad parenting, they should consider birth complications, potential brain damage in childhood, and possible infections as a probable contributor to ADHD. Studies show that family environments contribute to a certain extent to the child's ADHD. Excessive time on video games cannot cause ADHD. Having kids spend excessive amounts of time on their consoles can disrupt their sleep, interfere with their development, both intellectually and socially, and make them more distracted at school.

#5-You cannot have ADHD because you seem fine.

People with ADHD do not have a visible impairment. Most of the time, they would have developed a coping mechanism to help them cope with ADHD and compensate for their shortcomings. This does not mean that people with ADHD do not face daily struggles, but it just means not everyone can see these struggles. ADHD does not have a noticeable disability or anything that people can see, like a bandage or a tattoo saying, "I have ADHD." So, it's often easier for people to criticize because they have no idea what they're talking about.

#6-You cannot have ADHD because you get good grades.

People with ADHD can be gifted too. Contrary to what most people believe, if someone with ADHD is pursuing a college degree that interests them, they are likely to not only succeed but excel. They can hyper-focus all their time and energy, making them some of the best in class. Many successful people who have ADHD have made it in the business industry, became famous actors or athletes, and come up with inventive ideas. Take Scott Kelly, an astronaut, and Bill Gates as an example. People with ADHD can struggle to be part of companies and corporate associations that fail to fit their needs, so they tend to become entrepreneurs or owners of small businesses, often with innovative ideas.

#7-You should be jumping off a wall if you truly have ADHD.

There are different types of ADHD. The most common are the main three types: hyperactivity impulsive type ADHD, inattentive type, and combination type. There are different approaches to this, and some researchers and psychiatrists divide ADHD into further categories. Although the hyperactive-impulsive ADHD type is the most common type in boys and the most occurring one, it is not the only one. Those who have the hyperactive type of ADHD may grow out of that symptom later in life, but it does not mean that their ADHD goes away. Girls often experience the inattentive type, and this can often go unnoticed. Hyperactivity can also be internalized, where the brain never stops working and the body is restless.

#8-Girls cannot have ADHD.

This myth is what leaves a lot of girls undiagnosed with ADHD or misdiagnosed. Both boys and girls can have ADHD. But because girls do not disturb in class and the type of ADHD they usually have can seem like they are more forgetful and lazy, they are not encouraged to be treated, but rather become labeled from a very young age. They might seem to be more daydreamy. ADHD in girls and women has only recently been recognized, and further scientific reports are focusing on the significant impairments they face, often to the same degree as boys. They are at a potential threat for many of the same coexisting disorders and impairments as men, including oppositional defiant disorder, behavioral disorder, academic and social disorders, driving difficulties, drug misuse, and mental health issues. Adolescent girls with ADHD are more likely than boys to have eating disorders, like anorexia and bulimia.

#9-Everyone is a little ADHD.

This myth is equally offensive as it is incorrect. People can experience moments of forgetfulness, but that does not make everyone suffer from ADHD. For ADHD to be diagnosed, manuals and guidelines require the individual to experience more than just one symptom, at least 5 to be exact, in two different environments, since childhood to the point where it interferes with their lives. Before getting to an ADHD diagnosis, individuals can be diagnosed or misdiagnosed with other conditions like depression, anxiety, or mood disorder. This is because someone with ADHD would experience other symptoms besides forgetfulness, impulsivity, hyper-focus, sleep disturbance, and restlessness. So this myth is best to be avoided to minimize offending someone who has ADHD.

#10-Medication cures ADHD

There is no cure for ADHD, much like diabetes, insulin, good eating habits, and exercise can help control the condition but not cure it. Medication can only go so far. Usually, a holistic approach is taken to help control ADHD, including therapy, meditation, and coaching, together with medication. ADHD drugs do not work the same for everyone; besides, usually, physicians give trials of medications before concluding which one works best, with the dosage and frequency. People with ADHD can confirm that once the medication is stopped, symptoms can return. Additionally, people with ADHD on medication can still face difficulties and struggle with certain symptoms of ADHD. Medication makes ADHD symptoms easier to manage. Stimulant medication is not the only option that works for ADHD. Your doctor will determine what is best for you, and there are more options besides stimulant medication.

#11-Medication turns ADHD kids into zombies.

The purpose of ADHD drugs is not to turn kids into zombies but to make ADHD symptoms more manageable and their lives less of a struggle. ADHD drugs can help kids achieve their full potential. It can help them focus on the right tasks at school or help them transition from one task to the next. Research has also been conducted on ADHD in different ethnic groups. To further contradict this myth, research shows that African-Americans and Hispanics are less likely to accept ADHD medication as treatment for their kids diagnosed with ADHD.

#12-ADHD is over-diagnosed.

There has been an increase in ADHD diagnosis, but this does not mean assessment is being done carelessly. Doctors and physicians use specific guidelines when assessing a potential ADHD individual, and they do so based on their based practice and resources. The increased numbers of ADHD diagnoses are attributed to the increased awareness about the disorder. More screenings are being done by doctors and pediatricians. Treatment options and diagnostic tools are becoming more available to more physicians.

#13- People with ADHD cannot focus.

It is evident that people with ADHD have trouble focusing, but that happens only when something does not interest them. If there is something they enjoy doing, they can not only focus, but they will over-focus, to the point where you cannot make them do anything else until they are exhausted and ready to stop. In adult life, this may affect employees at work. As an employed individual, you may be asked to complete different tasks, some of which are of interest and others you might find boring. Neurodiverse brains will dedicate most of their time and energy to the tasks they enjoy doing. The issue is not lacking focus but finding it difficult to shift their focus from one task to the next, especially if one task seems boring. So, people with ADHD can indeed focus.

#14-ADHD is a learning disability.

Symptoms of ADHD interfere with the learning process of the sufferer, but it does not impede learning skills like reading, working on math problems, or writing. With that said, this does not mean that kids with ADHD cannot benefit from adjustments at school. This goes for people with ADHD at work, especially if they just started their career; on-the-job learning experience can be more challenging if they have ADHD.

Education and awareness is the only thing that can help people understand this condition and give it the attention and credit it deserves to facilitate the lives of people with ADHD.

Chapter 32:
ADHD Q&A

I f you have ADHD, you probably have questions all the time and seek to-the-point answers to help explain your symptoms and feelings. Here are some of the frequently asked questions relating to ADHD, whether you are a woman suspecting to have ADHD or have been diagnosed with ADHD:

1.   What is ADHD?

Attention deficit hyperactivity disorder (ADHD) is a neurodevelopmental disorder that lasts a lifetime. In more than three-quarters of cases, symptoms persist into adulthood. ADHD is distinguished by developmental abnormalities in inattention, impulsivity, and hyperactivity.

2.   What is the difference between ADHD and ADD?

ADD means an individual has attention deficit disorders but does not experience hyperactivity as a symptom. Remember, there are different types of ADHD, and one of them does not have hyperactivity as its main symptom. ADD is a term that was created to better describe those who suffer from the inattentive type of ADHD. Think of ADHD as an umbrella term.

3.   What is executive function?

This refers to one of the brain functions that work on activating, organizing, and managing other functions. This helps people evaluate their actions and make decisions. This is one of the symptoms of ADHD where most would experience executive dysfunction and have trouble organizing and making informed decisions.

4.   How is ADHD diagnosed?

ADHD is diagnosed in various ways, and it all depends on the resources available to your physician or doctor. There are general guidelines that help specialists diagnosed ADHD in a simple clinical setting through assessment and evaluation. Others may have brain imaging equipment available to them and may take different approaches to diagnose you. Ultimately the guidelines are the same for everyone. To be diagnosed with ADHD, you must experience more than 5 symptoms of ADHD since childhood in two or more different environments. Assessment is done with the neurotypical individual and their close relatives to be able to gather more information about their childhood at home and their learning experience at school.

5.   How does one find a mental health doctor to help diagnose my symptoms?

It is important to seek qualified and licensed professionals to help diagnose you with ADHD if you suspect you suffer from it. Ensure that the person you go to has had experience in the field and has worked with individuals with ADHD before. This depends on the availability of such professionals in your area and health insurance coverage. Many psychiatrists and therapists chose to specialize in different areas in the field like anxiety, depression, abuse, and ADHD. Find someone you are comfortable working with and someone you feel can help you diagnose yourself. Neurologists, physicians, general practitioners, and therapists can diagnose ADHD. Pediatricians can also do ADHD assessments in the case of children. Once you are diagnosed, you might be referred for different types of treatments like coaching and therapy. Ensure you feel comfortable with these professionals as well and ask about their experience in the field.

6.   Is there a connection between obesity and ADHD?

Because people with ADHD often suffer from impulsivity, they might binge eat or fall into unhealthy eating habits. Some ADHDers spend a lot of time indoors or playing video games, with little to no physical activity. This can all contribute to obesity and unhealthy lifestyles. This obstacle can be overcome by seeking help from a qualified nutritionist who can help you meal plan, make healthy eating choices, and keep you accountable for regular physical activity that can, in turn, help you manage your condition and help you keep a healthy weight.

7.   Are there any other conditions that can occur with ADHD?

Most people with ADHD can have at least one coinciding condition. Symptoms of ADHD may hide these disorders like anxiety and depression. Your doctor can determine whether to treat your coexisting condition first before your ADHD or whether treating your ADHD can help control your other conditions.

8.   How can my ADHD be treated?

You need to start by getting diagnosed. Once diagnosed, your doctor can determine what further assistance and treatment you required.

ADHD treatment varies from parenting advice, medication, coaching, counseling, cognitive behavioral therapy, and education about ADHD.

9.   Can my medication be prescribed electronically or over the phone?

This can vary from country to country. Non-stimulant medication can often be prescribed via refills over the phone and is easier to dispense. Stimulant medication, however, needs monthly prescriptions because it is a controlled substance. This is done to avoid substance abuse. Having access to stimulant medications is possible if you are under the care of a professional, and when taken as prescribed, this can help control your ADHD symptoms. Stimulant medication may require more commitment in terms of keeping appointments, getting your insurance to cover for it, and making sure you have prescriptions ready for your next month's supply.

10.   Doesn't ADHD affect only children?

One-third of children who exhibit ADHD symptoms as kids can continue to experience ADHD symptoms into adulthood. For adults and children to be diagnosed with ADHD, they must meet criteria issued by the medical board that controls the country you find yourself in.

11. Is there a relation between smoking and ADHD?

Adolescents with ADHD can have a higher risk of cigarette use than those who do not have ADHD. Smoking is more occurrent in adults with

ADHD also. Those who have ADHD and smoke may have difficulty quitting.

12. Is it safe for women to take stimulant medication to treat their ADHD if they are pregnant or planning to be?

Stimulant medication and pregnancy is not a study done in clinical trials; therefore, research and safety are lacking. This is solely dependent on your doctor and gynecologist. Ideally, if you plan to become pregnant and have ADHD that is being treated with stimulant medication, you should start discussing your options before getting pregnant. This can help you understand the pros and cons of having stimulant medication whilst pregnant, may decide to explore other options, and determine whether you intend to continue your treatment throughout the pregnancy. You may be able to seize medication before your pregnancy, so if there are any side effects you are not willing to risk, they can be avoided. This is a decision you are most likely to take with your physician and partner after some deliberation.

13. Should I let the people at work know I have ADHD?

This can put you in a pickle. Employers may not be obliged to make accommodations for an individual unless they have disclosed their special ability. The employee may feel discriminated against as soon as he or she discloses their ADHD. Ideally, you weigh in your options and determine whether you need accommodations because if you do not, it can be useless disclosing. If you already do a great job at work and your position is not at stake because your superiors think you complete your duties as you should, then disclosing your ADHD won't make a

247

difference and can be avoided. If you feel like disclosing can have you discriminated against, then ideally, you do not disclose.

On the other hand, if not disclosing means you lose your job because you cannot complete your duties, you should consider disclosing. If you might get fired because your superiors think you are not working hard enough, but the reason for your struggle is your ADHD, then you may consider disclosing it. Disclosing your ADHD does not mean you put yourself in a bad light, but rather highlight your strengths so you are assigned tasks that best highlight your abilities instead of leaving you struggling to complete something you cannot do by yourself or without having accommodations. Accommodations need to be fair to the rest of the team and can vary from having your own space to being allowed to work with headphones to cancel out background noise. A great employer who is proud to have you on their team will accommodate your needs and encourage you to reach the best version of yourself. If your work environment is a difficult one to accommodate and despite your disclosure, you are still being assigned tasks that you struggle to complete with no guidance or assistance, then you may need to consider a career change that better fits your abilities.

14. Can women with ADHD be successful?

Success is subjective, and whatever you view as successful may not be the same criteria for others. Success needs to be defined as the best version of oneself, whether they have ADHD or not. But to answer your question, YES, women with ADHD can and are becoming successful. Take Karina Smirnoff, a professional dancer, Mary-Kate Olsen, an award-winning actress, and Lisa Ling, a journalist who was diagnosed with ADHD at age 40. These are all women with ADHD who have become successful. ADHD can get in the way of your life, but treating it and educating yourself and those around you about it can make you reach your goals easier than expected.

15. What is the best advice you can give to women and young girls with ADHD?

If you feel like you might have ADHD, do not be afraid to speak up about your feeling and symptoms. If you feel like your current diagnosis of depression or anxiety is not the right one for you, seek a second opinion. Make sure you chose a physician you feel comfortable with and is a professional. Educating yourself and getting diagnosed is the starting point of an easier journey to life with ADHD. This condition cannot stop you from enjoying life, but if you understand the change your life needs to better fit your ADHD, you can be successful. Therapy and getting the right help can help you feel less sabotaged by your guilt and fear.

16. What are the most common misdiagnosed conditions to mask ADHD?

ADHD in women is often mistaken for anxiety, depression, and mood disorders. At a young age, they may be perceived as dreamy and lazy when they would be trying their best.

17. Why is it so hard for women to get diagnosed with ADHD?

As young girls, they would not disrupt their classmates and would allow a lesson to go on as planned. A boy with ADHD, usually the hyperactive-impulsive type, would not allow this and can be referred by their schoolteachers for treatment. If a girl misses her homework weeks on end, she is sent home with a note to the parents or guardians. She can be seen as lazy and not trying hard enough. As they grow older, women with ADHD can feel depressed or anxious, and when seeking medical assistance, they can often be misdiagnosed.

18. Do ADHD symptoms vary significantly in women than in men?

Women usually have the inattentive type of ADHD, and the symptoms do vary because most of the men have the hyperactive-impulsive type. There are some universal symptoms that both men and women with ADHD experience. They may both be chronically late, be impulsive, experience emotional dysregulation, be forgetful, and often misplace or lose things.

19. Do hormone changes affect ADHD in women?

Yes, ADHD is greatly affected by hormone changes in women. Because estrogen levels vary during puberty and menopause, ADHD symptoms can worsen or improve during a woman's lifetime. High estrogen levels can lighten ADHD symptoms, but during menstruation and later during menopause, ADHD symptoms can worsen. Menopause naturally makes a woman forgetful and confused, so having ADHD does not help.

20. Can a woman manage a job, her household, and a family if she has ADHD and does not take stimulant medication?

Women are asked to complete many tasks and are assigned a lot of duties as the organizers in society. Everyone can manage the same situation differently, so there is no one correct answer. One may feel like meditation and therapy are enough to manage their ADHD because they are surrounded by family members that understand and strive to make a household that is ADHD-friendly. Others may strive at work with the help of coaching and accommodations from their superiors because they happen to be at the right employment and have a good support system. But this may not be the situation for everyone. A single mother with ADHD, who also has a kid with ADHD, may struggle to manage her symptoms and duties without stimulant medication. She may require therapy, coaching, accommodations, and occasionally some medical treatment to help subside her symptoms and keep up with her demanding life. The ideal situation is to try whatever you think works for you, and if that is enough and you feel like you are making progress, you can keep doing what you are doing. There is no shame in asking for medication or contact your therapist out of your scheduled sessions.

21. Will getting diagnosed change my life?

Educating yourself and those around you can help you live a better life with ADHD. If you are not diagnosed, you cannot get the treatment you need, and if you need accommodations at work or from those around you, you cannot get them because no one knows what you are struggling with, not even yourself. Getting diagnosed is not labeling you but making you aware of the situation.

Conclusion

A s of now, there is very little information on ADHD in women since only a few studies have been conducted on this population. Women have recently been diagnosed and treated with ADHD, and today, the majority of what one believes about this population is based on the scientific expertise of mental health specialists who have spent considerable time counseling women. ADHD in small children is often overlooked, the reasons for which remain unknown, and often females are not evaluated until they are adults. Occasionally, a woman becomes aware of her ADHD after one of her children receives a diagnosis. When she explores ADHD, she notices a plethora of parallel cases of herself. Few women seek care for ADHD because their lives are out of control; their finances may be in disarray; their administrative job and record-keeping are often ineffectively overseen; they may struggle futilely to stay aware of the demands of their positions; and they may feel much less prepared to stay aware of the day-by-day tasks of meals, food, and life overall. Different women are more successful because they are isolated from all their ADHD, fighting bravely to remain mindful of increasingly problematic demands by working late into the evening and investing their spare time trying to "get coordinated." If a woman's life is clearly in disarray or she can hide her struggles, she often presents herself as overwhelmed and exhausted.

Although research into ADHD in women lags behind that in men, more clinicians are finding important issues and co-occurring symptoms in women with ADHD. Women with ADHD may be prone to binge eating, alcohol abuse, and chronic sleep deprivation. Women with ADHD also feel dysphoria, severe sadness, and tension issues, as well as troublesome and anxiety symptoms like men with ADHD. Regardless, women with ADHD tend to have more emotional suffering and have poorer mental self-esteem than men with ADHD. Women diagnosed with ADHD in adulthood are more likely to have burdensome side effects, to be more pushed and restless, to have a more external locus of control, to have poorer morale, and to be more locked in adopting practices that are feeling-oriented than task-situated. According to studies, having a parent with ADHD puts a strain on the whole family. However, women may experience more anxiety than men because they are more responsible for their homes and children. Furthermore, ongoing research suggests that husbands of women with ADHD are less tolerant of their partner's ADHD than spouses of men with ADHD. Persistent pressure harms women with ADHD, affecting their mental health. Women that experience chronic stress, such as that associated with ADHD, are more vulnerable to illnesses associated with chronic stress, such as fibromyalgia. As a result, it is becoming increasingly clear that the lack of proper diagnosis and treatment of ADHD in women is a critical public health problem.

If you have made it this far, a situation or two must have appealed to you. You most probably have so much in common with the practical examples brought to light. ADHD has been defined, and the different types have been outlined to facilitate the process for potentially undiagnosed or misdiagnosed women with ADHD. There is no denying that women with ADHD are misunderstood and overlooked in society. The idea is not to take the spotlight away from men and young boys with ADHD but rather shed light on women and their ADHD.

Addressing the main concerns for women with ADHD means no stone is left unturned. ADHD needs to be discussed and acknowledged in all walks of life, working women, mothers and mothers-to-be, and women going into menopause. ADHD cannot be cured, but it can be managed. Understanding cues the body gives off can help women keep an eye out for potential ADHD symptoms. Getting the right diagnoses can often mean scouting around for the best medical advice and seeking a practitioner you feel comfortable with, who also happens to have the right experience and sources to diagnose you. Women with ADHD require assistance and support throughout their lives. Some may have the luxury of having a great support system, making things easier for them. Others may need to be more perseverant to manage their lives and those of their children independently. Women with ADHD need to learn that all their failed tries and mistakes have shaped them and made them who they are. It does not stop at that. There are plenty of skills one can have and sources one can go to to help manage their finances, daily schedules, emotions, and relationships.

If a woman with ADHD feels out of place at work, she can now know better than blaming herself for not being good enough. Learn to use your best skills and overcome the weaker ones. Do not let your ADHD define you because you are more than your ADHD. Begin to enjoy yourself. To begin with, you have no power over your genetics. ADHD is a psychological condition, and self-control alone would not be enough to overcome genetics. Creativity, intuition, and resilience are also hereditary traits that are often associated with ADHD. Knowing all about this disorder can help everyone cope with it better. Help yourself understand that you need relief and assistance. This need fuels your creativity and allows you to excel in high-risk or high-stress situations.

Choose activities where your ADHD characteristics can support rather than hinder you, helping you feel accomplished and fulfilled. Know that you are unique and always remember ADHD doesn't make you less human; your brain just doesn't stick to the "acceptable" way of living set by society. Don't make ADHD an excuse but rather the fuel that empowers you to get all your heart desires. I believe in you!! Believe in yourself and GO GET IT!!!

Author's Note

Dear reader,

I hope you enjoyed my book.

Please don't forget to toss up a quick review on amazon, I will personally read it! Positive or negative, I'm grateful for all feedback.

Reviews are so helpful for self-published authors and your feedback can make such a difference for my book!

Thanks very much for your time, and I look forward to hearing from you soon.

Sincerely,

Roberta

Made in the USA
Columbia, SC
14 April 2025

56616831R00141